DAVID WALKING
WITH GRACE

Dr. Neal Boeder MD

David Walking with Grace:
Healing yourself, family, and society by laughing, loving, and learning.
Dr. Neal Boeder

Canadian Copyright No: 1205907
Date: 2023-09-01

www.nealboeder.com

1st Edition. 1st printing 2024

Cover Concept Design and Interior Design:
Steve Walters, Oxygen Publishing Inc.

Editor: Richard Tardif

Independently Published by
Oxygen Publishing Inc.
Montreal, QC, Canada
www.oxygenpublishing.com

ISBN: 978-1-990093-82-1
Imprint: Independently published

Dedication

To my daughter, as this book and the songs we know teach us that we never know what's around the bend in life. Your father is forever on your side[1]. May my story remind you in scary times; stand firm and remind yourself to do everything with love. Peace, be still when you are scared[2]. You know I am cheering you on[3]. This book is dedicated to you, those whose lives you will grace, and to my best friend who died before you were born…

Contents

Preface

**What's the difference between God and a doctor?
God doesn't think he's a doctor.**

B> ut this doctor isn't typical. I live every moment knowing I could die in an instant. My genetic heart condition makes my heart too big—so a sudden cardiac arrest could happen anytime. I have a scar on the left side of my chest from a defibrillator in my early 30s, serving as a daily reminder of my mortality. It's never been lost on me that my best friend died because his heart, like mine, was too big. I owe it to him, to my daughter, and many others to share my story of healing.

Are you or someone you love hurting? Like me, do you feel the weight of pain in our society? Are you searching for a way to help bring healing and restoration to those around you? If so, this book is for you. I invite you to embark on a unique and transformative journey. In a world often burdened by distress and strife, it can be easy to lose sight of the lighter side of life. Laughter, humility, and compassion possess remarkable healing powers that mend the deepest wounds and foster connections that transcend our differences. In this spirit, I intertwine humor and humility, offering a profound opportunity for personal growth and societal transformation.

I invite you to explore self-discovery. We can navigate the complexities of our lives with grace, resilience, and a renewed sense of purpose. Let us dismantle barriers, mend brokenness, and nurture the seeds of empathy. Join me in embracing the healing power of laughter, humility, and compassion. We can bring positive change and foster a compassionate and empathetic society.

In David Walking With Grace, we will laugh, love, and learn. We will transform hurt into hope. This book is about embracing vulnerability and sharing successes and failures. As a first-generation college graduate who became a physician, I will pull back the curtain to reveal my strengths and areas that require growth.

I've made mistakes. One of my early misdiagnoses was both laughable and understandable. I misinterpreted a rapidly growing mass on a 700-pound patient, believing it to be accessory legs for dancing. However, the patient was a cow giving birth. I was a four-year-old boy on my family's dairy farm. This experience humbled me and made me aware of my limitations in certain areas.

Over the next three decades, my family described me as proud and tough—traits passed down. However, I've also learned humility and understanding. Being humbled has allowed me to choose gentler words, listen attentively, and understand others. My daughter has witnessed this transformation, going from using harsh and loud words to speaking softly and listening.

My story wouldn't be complete without mentioning the scars I carry, both physical and emotional. I have faced numerous challenges throughout my journey including battling cancer twice, resulting in scars on each side of my neck and one on my chest from the defibrillator. My enlarged heart, instilled by my family as a sense of justice and willingness to help others, sometimes led me to anger and unjust assumptions. However, I've realized that anger doesn't bring about healing.

As a doctor, I understand the importance of living a healthy life. However, I reached a point where I struggled with my weight and self-image. I had to confront my weaknesses and strive for balance in my physical and mental well-being. By humbling myself and making necessary changes, I am gradually becoming a better person, physician, friend, father, and son.

I believe the best healers are those who have experienced hurt themselves. As someone who has faced cancer, depression, anxiety, and fractured relationships, I am committed to healing the brokenness in our society and individuals. Through my experiences as a parent, patient, and physician, I hope to offer insights and support to those recovering from physical, mental, or social pain.

Introduction

In my younger days I believed in Jesus, but mostly as a historical figure. I believed he died for our sins and loved us, but I didn't believe he was still doing miracles today. This time it's different. My faith muscle trained for over five years. I believe in the power of an Almighty to do miracles right here and now in my one-bedroom apartment. So instead of calling 911, I desperately pray that God stops this bleeding.

This wasn't a "test of God." It was out of faith but also from pure exhaustion. Even calling 911 means I must get up and be awake for the next few hours. I don't think I can even stay awake for that. Fighting fatigue hard, I fear I could fall asleep immediately. Faith and science are my guiding principles, so I set the alarm for ten minutes. I am not testing God. I believe faith must be coupled with action. I could fall asleep and still be bleeding. Praying I position myself in a "safe position," I lean forward and to the side on my couch, wrap pillows around me, and position myself so that any blood will hopefully not go into my airway where it could form a clot and kill me. My body is done, but my brain is fighting on. My spirit is calling on my savior. I am scared, tired, and hopeless.

I pray, and I close my eyes to think. If that alarm goes off and I'm still bleeding, I'm calling 911. The bleeding becomes worse. I'm calling 911. If I start coughing? I'm calling 911. Shortness of breath? I'm calling.... Ghostbusters. No, I'm not!

Just checking to see if you are paying attention!

It's 10 minutes till 911...

Chapter 1

Parenting: The Courage to Heal, Despite Fear

Parents prepare children for life's inevitable crises. Crises take many forms, such as cancer (I have had cancer twice), divorce (once), finances, the death of a loved one, or a life-changing injury. We all will experience a crisis.

The first time I prepared my daughter for a life crisis, she was under nine months old and in a swimming pool. I taught her about courage. When my daughter took infant swim classes, other parents held their infants briefly underwater and then up quickly. None of the infants were excited about this. Come to think about it, at age 43 I am not enthusiastic about somebody else dunking me.

The first few times we did it, she bawled intensely; she hated it. Some parents in the pool decided they would not continue to do it, not wanting to put their children through that unpleasant experience. I struggled briefly, for as much as I want to protect my daughter from unpleasantness in this world, some things are going to happen to her that I can't prevent: heartbreak, not landing that job or making the team, bullying, divorce, traumatic injuries, or worse. The pool was an opportunity for her to develop courage, going into a scary situation but coming out the other side better off. I continued dunking, but I smiled each time she came up, telling her how proud I was of her bravery. It was hard to see her scared, but after five or six times, she smiled. She briefly experienced hurting when she went under the water, but there was healing as she came up and saw her dad smiling, telling her how proud he was of her. That infant dunk helped her overcome the fear of the water. Now years later, she's a better swimmer than her parents!

First, she overcame her fear of the water. Without doing so, she could not have experienced joy when she came up. Learning to swim begins with the realization that something more significant than fear of water exists.

My childhood fear of water kept me from learning to swim. At four, I almost drowned and was left with a fear of the water. I graduated from high school without learning to swim. I didn't learn to swim until I was an adult. I wish I had known how to swim when I was younger; the hurt of water filling the lungs of this four-year-old boy turned into the healing of the man 30 years later while teaching his infant daughter to be courageous. She still has that courage because she sings, "I'm not gonna be afraid, cause these waves are only waves," with conviction every time the song *Peace Be Still* by Hope Darst[2] plays. She wasn't afraid in 2022 when a stranger dunked her in the water at Lake Johanna. She leaped into my arms after. Little did we know the green shirt I wore in the water that day would soon be stained in my blood. More on that later...

Fear is a wall to many things, preventing us from reaching our full potential. We may stay at that wall for just a moment, for months, or at that wall for years. Sometimes, it's a lifetime until we find the courage to realize something greater than fear exists on the other side.

Courage is often situational. People can be courageous in one area of life yet afraid in another. Soldiers may have the courage to charge into battle, but fear might prevent them from discussing mental health. A mother may have the courage to give birth and work two jobs for her children, but fear prevents taking time to heal her addiction. If you're that mother, soldier, or a person struggling with addiction or mental health, I hope you know I am cheering you on. I encourage you to listen to the lyrics in the song *Cheering You On*, by King and Country—I hope you don't dare give up. As the song says, "Gracious in the fight of it, Humble at the height of it, Choose to love despite it all. And when you're questioning the why of it, Rise up in the Light of it."

I'll be by your side in it all. I'm Cheering You On.

Courage is often associated with strength. Although related, there is a downside when we think about courage requiring strength. It puts us into a mindset of needing to conquer someone or something. Sometimes the most courageous acts are done in kindness or humility towards an enemy we don't defeat but instead, love or forgive. Something I taught my daughter is from Corinthians. "*Be on guard, stand firm in the faith. Be courageous, do everything in love.*" It reminds us to be ready; life can turn upside down instantly by one mistake; the text while driving that leads to a car accident, the angry words that cost you a job. With courage, we don't fight just for ourselves but for the least among us.

Hurting people, in their hurting, often hurts us. It's easy to pick up the emotional rock and throw it back, but everyone's healing starts with love. Trading insults has healed no relationship.

It takes courage to fight hate with love, bite your tongue, take deep breaths, and control your anger. Martin Luther King Jr. said, "Darkness cannot drive out darkness; only light can do that. Hate cannot drive out hate; only love can do that[4]."

Courage is showing love to someone who hurt you. In terms of sports, no one better exemplifies this than one of my heroes, Jackie Robinson[5]. Jackie Robinson, one of the all-time greatest Americans, famously broke baseball's color barrier in the 1940s. As the first African American in Major League Baseball, he was under a microscope. He was expected to perform exceptionally both athletically and emotionally. He did both by not retaliating when racist baseball players insulted him, threw baseballs at his head, and treated him terribly, hoping to provoke his anger. If they provoked it, and he allowed it to control his actions, the story would be about his violent reaction, not the cruelty that triggered it.

His courage came in calmness. In doing so, his love healed the hurt of their hate. In the movie *42*[6], there is a famous scene where Robinson says to Brooklyn Dodgers general manager Branch Rickey, "You want a player who doesn't have the guts to fight back?" to which Rickey responds, "NO, I want a player who has the guts NOT to fight back." Jackie thinks about it and says, "You give me a uniform, and you give me a number on my back, and I will give you the guts." It occurred to me while writing this book that as the first African American to play in major league baseball, Robinson didn't just get a number on his back; he got a target on his back too. Robinson's wife also knew this. They were both understandably nervous before his first game. Trying to calm his wife before he took to the diamond as the only black man on a field of white players, he famously told his wife,

"If you have trouble finding me, I will be the guy wearing 42," to lighten up that situation. Jackie knew he was about to experience hate from many white people. He needed to use humor, love, patience, and unimaginable courage to step onto a field with players who hated him. Some were on his team!

He didn't know that because of his ability to respond to evil with love and anger with patience, he was about to become a hero to this white man from rural America that wouldn't be born for another 30 years. This white man can't write about courage without including Jackie. Imagine baseballs thrown at your head and horrendous insults in your ears. You must be calm and focused enough to hit a round ball traveling at 90 mph. Then the moment you do, adrenaline flows and you run at full speed around the bases, only to end with a pair of metal cleats spiked into you.

His anger was entirely justified; that first year he somehow turned the other cheek and, in so doing, defeated the color barrier. Hearts and minds shifted when they saw him look such brutality in the eye and not retaliate. He didn't change every mind, but many enemies became allies. His grace took the hurting baseball inflicted on his fellow African Americans and healed instead. Jackie's love integrated baseball decades before the rest of the country caught up. He didn't know that some of those racist parents yelling at him had children next to them, who because of him, would see the world differently than their parent's generation. They would be future freedom riders. He didn't know that his number 42 would be the first number ever to be retired by *every* team in a professional sport league. He didn't realize that baseball would dedicate an entire day every year to his honor. He didn't know that on that day, in a sport where everyone used to be white, every player wears number 42.

It is called Jackie Robinson Day and the best part of this is that history recalls Jackie, and virtually no one remembers the names of those who showed him hate. History will reflect the healing of his love and overcoming the hurt of hate.

He didn't know that almost 80 years later, I would wake up in a hospital bed in pain. Yet, I would smile when I saw on TV that it was his wife, Rachel Robinson's 100th birthday. Just seeing her on TV would be enough to ease the pain a surgeon's knife in my neck had caused just a few hours earlier.

Fear comes from different sources. We root some in past trauma. Some are rational, some irrational. Jackie Robinson's fear of a baseball thrown at his head was rational. Even more rational is my daughter's fear of my cooking! I cook best with a credit card. Beyond this, watch out; I am dangerous when left alone in a kitchen.

Fear, like anger, can control our behavior and cause overreactions. It holds us back, tears apart relationships, and hurts us. Take for example, someone's fear of admitting to neighbors that their spouse is an alcoholic. That fear can hinder them from getting a support team to battle an addiction. What if that neighbor, unknown to you, has ten years of sobriety and could mentor your spouse? What if instead of drinking beer at the BBQ, they drink a Pepsi or offer a ride to AA?

To illustrate this point, baseball player Josh Hamilton's[7] story is one I have shared with countless patients. The Tampa Bay Rays drafted him first overall in 1999. As an 18-year-old, he had a bright future and a 3.96 million dollar signing bonus. His baseball career started promising, but Josh soon fell into addiction. He became known for car accidents, failed drug tests, and failed attempts at rehab.

By 2004 he was out of baseball. The book on his career appeared closed. It's clear the wolves were hunting him down. As in the Needtobreathe's song, *Hard Love*[8], he started "trading punches with the heart of darkness." After three years out of baseball he picked himself up and eventually would get his life back, hitting 200 home runs in his MLB career.

Most people miss the little caveat that Josh was very public about his struggles. It takes courage to admit your problems, but when you overcome the fear, you allow people to surround you that know about you, and can help. If you're hurting and afraid to tell others, they can't help in your healing. If I am a loyal friend to someone like Josh, I can now meet him for coffee instead of happy hour, and spend New Year's Eve playing cards at a house rather than in a bar. A loyal friend wants to help, but they don't know how unless you overcome the fear of telling them what demons you are struggling with. The thing is, we all wrestle with some type of demon. It may be an addiction, financial problems, depression, an eating disorder, or an affair. If you google

Josh's life, you will see it hasn't always been perfect; like many addicts, he has had relapses—periods of sobriety, and who knows how his story ends. I know he's got a chance; he's got people cheering him on, and he didn't die at age 23 when the book appeared closed. He is still in the game because his fear of embarrassment and judgment didn't prevent him from sharing his struggles. His story is about helping others heal, as now they are aware of one prong to use in a multi-pronged attack. We will discuss more of this in chapter ten, but for now I will leave you with this thought: you might not be a professional athlete, but don't let the fear of embarrassment prevent you from getting the help you need to heal. If you are struggling because of physical pain, an affair, financial, spiritual, mental, or whatever your affliction, there are people in your life who want to help. Something greater than fear exists. I believe in you; I might not know you, but I know there is a reason you decided to read this book. Deep down, you know you are meant for greater things, so just like Jackie and Josh, don't let fear hold you back.

The fear of being hurt again can lead a divorced person to sit on the sidelines and never meet a loving companion for a new start. On the other end, fear might cause someone to stay in an abusive relationship, because when afraid of starting over we accept less than what we are worth.

Fear, like anger, lives in the parts of the brain called the amygdala and temporal lobe. If you didn't go to medical school, or maybe you're a close friend who missed a class or two in med school because you were busy winning your fantasy sports league when you should have been in class, it's okay, I will explain. P.S. If you're considering writing a book, it's a great way to poke fun at your trusted friends and family.

•

The amygdala is a walnut-shaped portion of our brain; the temporal lobe sits on the side and lower portion of the brain. These are not the parts of the brain we want predominating over major decisions. We want our frontal lobe in the captain's seat. These parts of the brain stimulate knee-jerk reactions that make us seem more like apes than humans. Our frontal lobe is where we more rationally plot a wiser course in life. Our emotions love to jump out of "nowhere" and grab control. You might be like me; too often those emotions took over. Did the damage by speaking out from emotions when insulted. The frontal lobe knows it's foolish to respond in anger with harsh words; much wiser to use gentle comments. For most of my life, my frontal lobe picked up the pieces of the mess other parts of my brain made. You might feel helpless, but I've been there. I can tell you there is hope. Change is possible, and this hope is based upon good science mixed with a bit of faith. It's a hope based on a journey out of the darkness I am walking through today.

So, what's the science? I mentioned being someone who wore my emotions on my sleeve. I thought that was just who I was. Thankfully, there is a way that the frontal lobe can wrestle away the controls from those emotional parts of the brain. Our brain has this beautiful thing called neuroplasticity. Think of it this way: we don't grow new brain cells, but we can learn to use specific processing patterns more and others less. Here is how I think of it: we have roads in our brain, like freeways, that can rapidly move lots of information. We built most of our current processing and reactions over the years to become efficient. These pathways are the first choice for transporting information along the brain's superhighway.

Other parts of the brain are like side streets, narrow with stop signs. Things move slower and less often. Is this road our default route? It might be the better way to go, but it's not traveled on as often or as quickly as that highway. The beauty of our design is that we can, over time, turn these healthy side streets into information (and behavioral) superhighways. The new ways can become fast routes we go to first that carries most of the traffic in our mind. Those unhealthier routes suddenly develop stop signs as we build these healthier side streets.

How do we do this? It isn't easy, but it's worth it. It lets your family and friends see a more patient side of you. The kind side of you wins out. It heals torn relations with your parents, coworker, or a former best friend. It saves the need to apologize. It turns shouting into laughter when you diffuse the situation with humor, instead of criticizing. It starts by first deciding you maybe, just maybe, want to be ever so slightly better. This is despite the fact it's the other person causing all the problems. After all, you're sure you are already perfect; I mean, I know I am, or perhaps maybe we are both ALMOST perfect!

Next, find healthy resources to help you see different life paths. The less traveled but healthier road compared to that superhighway taking you repeatedly to a place you didn't want to end up. These resources may be professional; they may be healthy friends or coworkers. Often it will be both. Who is that person in your life that is always calm, making wise decisions, financially secure, or in a healthy relationship? Sometimes, it's someone obvious; other times, it's someone we lost contact with, like a former mentor at work or a previous neighbor. Reconnect, and don't be afraid to ask them how they do it; most people are happy to point others to the things that bring light into their life. If you want what they have in terms of peace, stability in relationships, etc., then walking the road they walk is a good place to start.

The next one is the hard one. You must be ready to hear the answer, so ensure you are in a good place. When you are ready, ask them to be honest about your blind spots. We all have them, things others see in us that we don't see in ourselves. Pick five people in your life and tell me something they repeatedly do that is annoying. If you find flaws in even one of them, trust me, they see areas for potential growth in you. If all five are perfect, then call me. I want to hang out with your friends and family! After all, I have been looking for other perfect people besides myself. If only… if only!

Building healthier roads of thought in life starts with putting in the effort. Instead of watching Monday Night Football, it's going to a counselor. Instead of spending time at a bar for guys or girls night, it's reading a self-help book. Instead of the ENTIRE weekend dedicated to kids' sporting events, it's squeezing in an hour for Church (even if online) or an inspirational podcast. Our faith or a support group can meet you on an iPhone at 9 p.m. after a game on Friday night. It might be 30 minutes of walking instead of scrolling social media. On the drive to work, instead of top 20 music. Maybe a financial advisor's self-help audiobook, or a station with uplifting lyrics and conversations. On that stressful day, when you want that third drink to relax, meditate instead. I am not knocking football, beer, or cheese curds at happy hour. I have enjoyed them all. Besides, if I were knocking beer or cheese curds, I would be in trouble; Wisconsin is my neighboring state. Miller Park?[11] Cheeseheads[11] at stadiums? I mean, Wisconsin exports some great things to Minnesota other than Brett Favre. But everything is in moderation, including moderation.

Enough football talk; once you find helpful engineers to show you how to build a better road, start laying down new pavement. Start capturing those thoughts before they race on the freeway and send them down a healthier side street. At first, it will be a mixed bag. You get it right a few times at first and wrong even more times. This is part of the process. Don't beat yourself or give up; it's normal. You must grab a thought going 100 mph and force it to turn down a new road. It won't be intuitive. You won't notice it until you're halfway to destruction.

Also, realize that even if others have been going and thinking the same way for years, you can still be going the wrong way. After all, misery loves company. Sometimes improving means not only new ways of thinking or doing, but also the new voices we give priority to. When we try to change and be healthier, it's not uncommon for old friends/family/colleagues to resist. Just have one more drink; who needs yoga? Why are you listening to a boring podcast, etc? It's not that we have to give up old friends or family, but how much credence and weight we give to healthy vs. unhealthy voices in our life that makes an impact. When change happens, these old roads and new roads sometimes compete for our thoughts, which route will they go down.

I had this situation once. A patient had frustrated the hospital physicians and nursing staff hours before being admitted to my care. People were exasperated because we were disproportionately spending time on this one patient, not because of the patient's medical complexity or needs, but because of their behavioural actions in misleading people. A trusted nurse at her wit's end came and asked me, "Straighten this mess out!"

We were at the end of a long shift; I already had 11 hours in and could have left the hospital two hours earlier. I was still there because I cared, sometimes too much. I bleed with my patients; when they hurt, I hurt; when they rejoice, I rejoice. I have to keep a certain objectivity. Nevertheless, I care for them deeply. She was a caring nurse, but we were exhausted and irritated. An adult patient acting immaturely is frustrating, especially when it distracts from other good deeds we need to do. The American healthcare system is broken and as a whole, cares more about profits than patients. Understaffing and overworking is expected, with less time to do the important work. So when additional effort is sucked up with things like this, we get burned out. I had a simple justified solution, but not necessarily as kind as the other options I could have deployed.

Halfway down the hallway with the nurse toward this patient's room, a thought popped into my head, "What do you do to the least of these…" then another, "How do you treat someone who can do nothing for you?" I remember the lines from an old Garth Brooks song about being kind; even when we can't save everyone, we can save one. The lyrics continue, "It's not the world that I am changing; I do this so this world will know that it can't change me.[12]"

I took a deep breath. Was I supposed to take the longer, kinder approach when the honest and direct approach was justified? Either approach was ok. I had already addressed the medical issues. It wasn't my job to explore social problems. None of the other physicians had. Why should I go down a different road, or why did it have to be at this hour? At least a dozen physicians had seen this patient in the preceding weeks. They had all made a similar medical diagnosis that I agreed with. None of them had time to tackle the social issues. I was tired, and my old information superhighway would get me some food when I hadn't eaten in 10-plus hours, and allow me to go home, fall into bed for barely seven hours of sleep, and then be back again to start all over.

This new road was going to mean little sleep tonight. I struggled with this, and the nurse initially wanted me to take the old road. Alas, I jumped off the superhighway in my mind. Instead, I turned down a small side street with poorly lit signs that required genuine effort. Neuroplasticity meant I wasn't as familiar with this path but could become more familiar. Like a new trail that initially has tall grass and branches in the way, as you walk it more a dirt path and cleared branches appear making it easier each time until you have a well-traveled, newer way of thinking.

Over the following 90 minutes, this vexed nurse and physician explored this patient's social dynamics. We shared stories of fear, anger and frustration. The nurse and I built a therapeutic relationship with the patient, and now it was possible to overcome these issues. It was a powerful healing. We were glad we went the extra mile. I do not know what happened ultimately, but I know we gave this patient a chance to take a different road; if indeed that patient did. I can't tell you when you are learning a new way in life, not everyone will want to follow or take it.

Sometimes the victory lies not in the outcome but in the designation you took. Now your brain knows that route just a little better. The street signs are clearer to see. It's a little easier and faster to get to the frontal lobe of your brain next time. The frontal lobe is better able to be in control of those emotions. Now given a more zany humor and goofball personality, some people wonder if I have a frontal lobe, but I do. Many are surprised to hear this, but they saw it on an MRI. I have pictures to prove it!

Chapter 2

Forgiveness: It's About Us, Not Them

I have respect for those who stand up to someone who hurt them. The strength demonstrated in such a situation is admirable. I admire those with the strength to testify and ensure individuals are held accountable for their actions. It's courageous to establish boundaries, move on to another relationship, or speak with someone so they no longer hurt you physically, emotionally, or financially

However, what if, in addition to showing such strength, you choose to respond with love instead of anger toward the perpetrator? It is incredibly inspiring when individuals display such strength and embrace love and compassion for their fellow human beings. These genuine men and women heroes fearlessly declare, "I am not afraid of you. Despite the pain you have caused me, you will not diminish my love for others."

They recognize that although you can inflict harm, you cannot force them into the depths of hatred. They stand tall with strength and love, refusing to allow bitterness to replace kindness in their hearts. It is a powerful testament to their character and resilience.

These aren't easy things to do, but they are courageous. Someone who's hurt us is not necessarily someone who "deserves to be forgiven." To the person reading this who might have been a victim of sexual assault, domestic violence, or lost a loved one to a drunk driver, lost a marriage, a job or whatever pain you are dealing with, please know my heart goes out to you. I understand why you may not want to forgive them. I also see why you don't feel like you should or need to, but bear with me.

I understand they might not even ask for forgiveness or think they did anything wrong. Forgiveness allows us to heal fully. You can hold someone accountable, have boundaries with them, and let go of your anger. Two of my heroes managed to do both of these things. The first was Brandt Jean in a story of mistaken apartments. The story caught my eye as the building I lived in at the time had identical layouts on each floor. I had inadvertently tried to unlock the apartment directly below me once when I didn't realize I had gotten off on the wrong floor. I also had someone try to unlock my door until they realized they were on the wrong floor. So when I heard about a series of unfortunate events leading to someone killing an innocent man in his own home due to mistaken apartments, I read more.

Brandt Jean was wronged and forever hurt when Amber Guyger, an off-duty police officer, killed his brother. In brief, she thought she was going into her apartment but was instead going into someone else's. An unforgivable error led to a young, innocent man, Brandt Jean's brother, dying. In a telling video, Brandt Jean testified in court on behalf of his innocent brother. What he did at the end of his testimony was shocking, powerful, and one of the greatest acts of forgiveness I have seen. After testifying, he asked the judge if he could hug this woman. He wanted her to know that although she had made a mistake and justice needed to be served, he would also show

Use the QR code to see the video.

her love and forgiveness. That hug was probably one of the most powerful hugs in the history of humankind.

Corrie Ten Boom suffered another case of "unforgivable" atrocities. Her family helped Jewish people escape Nazis persecution during the Holocaust. They were caught and sent to the Ravensbrück concentration camp. Her book, *The Hiding Place*[13], recounts the story of what they suffered. In the Alpha course[14], she is quoted about interacting with a former guard from a Nazi prison camp. This guard was responsible for the terrible atrocities that she had experienced as a child, as well as the death of her sister. Decades later, when they met, he asked her for forgiveness. She explained how at first, she was not able to forgive him, but in beautiful examples of the combination of courage, strength, and love, she explains how she was able to forgive him. That love was stronger than hate; hearing her describe this is worth a google search.

Use the QR code to see the video.

Much of what I've talked about regarding forgiveness has been related to the person who needs the forgiving, who did the atrocities.

Forgiving someone is as much about helping me as it is about helping them. If I am not forgiving someone, I'm holding on to anger about what they did. Often that anger was justified. I won't tell you that feeling anger is wrong. Anger is an emotion, normal and morally neutral. If we control, it can lead to great change. If it controls us, it leads to horrible things. Anger that we hold onto starts to erode other parts of our life. It takes away happiness; it carries over into other situations where we blow up at someone over the slightest issue. We go from someone angry about ONE thing to becoming a person who is angry at almost everything. Anger controls us like a lion waiting to pounce on whoever makes the slightest mistake.

In your social media friends, coworkers, classmates, and family, you will find that person who is always angry about something. It seems relatively minor, or their response appears out of proportion. It's not just about a particular issue; it's anger from other issues that have grown over time.

When we carry around anger, what we carry around is an emotional Jack in the Box constantly being tightened; it will eventually burst out of us. Innocent people we love or work with or run across in the store become the ones who unwittingly turn that crank. Suddenly, we blow up at them. Letting go of anger has helped me not let that Jack in the Box control my responses.

In that same Alpha course, Nicky Gumbel, the presenter, describes still being angry with someone as allowing them to rent space in your brain for free. You are giving them control over your thoughts. You're not just renting a specific space in your brain; eventually, they invade other areas of your brain and life. That initial anger is brief if we let it go. If we hold onto that anger, it grows and controls us. If we allow this anger to grow, it becomes like cancer. It takes up more than just internal thoughts. It moves to our heart, which becomes hardened. Instead of spending a few minutes thinking about that person or situation, this anger moves to our eyes and how we see the world. It invades our mouths and what we say to others. It invades our ears so we can't hear apologies. It eventually becomes who we are!

Thankfully there is a treatment for anger. Unlike cancer, treatment works no matter how advanced the stage of your anger. Like cancer treatment it takes time, with multiple modalities and experts. Instead of surgery, chemo, or radiation, you may need counseling, medication, yoga, relaxation, support groups, and prayers to defeat invasive anger. Instead of letting your enemy who hurt you invade every part of your life, you defeat your enemy by kicking that anger out. I've had cancer in my body, but I also had anger invade my thoughts, eyes, ears, and heart. It was justified, but letting go of it was better than it invading me. I have learned to fight back against it. Like shrinking a tumor, I learned to shrink how long anger lasts. I have taken control back from those "enemies" that hurt me. They no longer control my emotions. You know you have won when you can have compassion for those former "enemies." Taking control back means I chose love over anger. I would rather laugh, love, and improve the world for my and my enemies' kids. After all, this city, country, and planet are still the places we all call home.

We will rise or fall together; love will build us up. Anger wants to tear us down; let's not let it. Besides Jackie Robinson, another hero of mine, David, did this. You know the David vs. Goliath story, yup, that one. His greatest victory over an enemy in battle isn't the famous one we've all heard. No, that's just a teaser; the really good part is what he does (and doesn't do) to his enemy Saul years later; now that is the most exceptional but less known victory. That, my friend, is worth a read.

Chapter 3

A Blood Soaked Shirt.
This Patient's Three Nights in July

Science is a critical element of how I explain things. As a physician, science is how I heal. Sometimes people describe miracles that they don't understand, but as a physician, there is a logical medical explanation. I advocate for people to use modern medicine in their healing. I am not just a physician, I am also a patient.

At 43, during the summer of 2022, I received the distressing news that I had again developed head and neck cancer. I went through it in 2017. Surprisingly, this was not a recurrence of my previous cancer but a completely new one on the opposite side. It is an exceptionally rare occurrence, happening only to about one in every 2,000-3,000 individuals. Unfortunately, luck was not on my side this time. My daughter witnessed the unsettling sight of her father undergoing surgery, resulting in matching scars on both sides of my neck, five years apart. Surgeries, chemotherapy, radiation, enduring pain, and significant weight loss consumed our summer. Our eagerly anticipated summer bucket list, which we create every year, had to be put on hold. The many conversations about life I had envisioned having with my daughter now hang in uncertainty. The amount of time we have left to spend together on this Earth is unclear. Little did I realize that this seemingly unbearable situation would transform into the most profound blessing of my life.

I completed surgery in mid-July; technically, my surgeon completed the surgery. I just took a long nap. Typical man, sleeping on the job while a talented woman does the work! My surgeon is kind, intelligent and skilled. I recommend her to anyone. She's so skilled I am helping her pay off her med school loans, one surgery at a time, every few years. She is going to need to name an exam room after me!

The surgery or nap was a tough one to wake up from, a lot of hurting but also a lot of healing. The kind nurse would give me pain meds to help and heal

me with empathy and kindness. We talked about families. She pulled up a song I asked her to. It comforted me, *Peace Be Still* by Hope Darst[2]. It reminded me of that day in the pool with my infant daughter. "I don't want to be afraid every time I face the waves." I was hurting, but the voice sang, "I'm not going to be afraid, Cause these waves are only waves, Peace be still, Say the words and I will." Years ago, I was trying to help my daughter be calm and understand she should face those waves when she went under the water. I wanted her to hear my voice and be calm. Now I was the scared child, being told I could face these waves. Just to be still. As I lay in pain, that song and conversation about life had as much to do with easing my pain as the pain meds.

Ten nights later, the most powerful healing in my life would occur.

The following week and a half was full of misery. Short on sleep; pain keeps me up. The previous radiation and surgery to my neck plus this round of surgery had produced so much tightness. I could barely open my mouth. Some might say it is good since I have a big mouth! It's almost impossible even to get a spoon in my mouth. The healing surgical wound in my throat severely limits the types of food I can have—Boost and shakes are it. I lost five to 10 pounds quickly. I lost even more sleep. I'm recovering from two separate surgeries. One is the tonsillectomy, and the other is a neck dissection to remove lymph nodes. Due to nerve damage my shoulder is unstable, weak, and hurts. My neck is tight, and on "good nights" I sleep for three to four hours at a time.

On July 29, ten days post-op, I woke up and my heart sank. My face, shirt, and pillow had dried blood on them. I had unknowingly bled in the middle of the night without waking up. I could've died. Bleeding in your throat is one way people with my type of cancer die. Still processing what happened and looking in the mirror, I read the words on my bloodstained green shirt. "Jesus saves." I laughed, saying, "Yes, yes, he does." As a physician, I explain most things as a scientist. Jesus wanted to clarify that this wasn't about science but about him.

My faith could believe Jesus healed me. The scientist in me couldn't let go. Bleeding from a surgical site in the back

Follow the QR code or visit www.nealboeder.com to see the colour pictures.

of my throat is extremely dangerous. In a sleeping position, blood goes back down and into the throat or airway. Aspirating blood is an emergency; clots can enter your airway.

I wondered if there was more bleeding than what I saw. The blood on my pillow and face had gone forward onto my shirt. Did more go to the back of my throat also? Where did the bleeding start? At the surgical site, most likely. Did I bite my tongue or lip? I couldn't see or feel a lip laceration.

I struggled with many things; was it a miracle? I was nervous about what others might say if I shared my experience. Was I supposed to share? This bleeding occurred on a Thursday night into Friday morning, the first night of my journey.

On the second night (post-op day 11), I went to the emergency room for swelling in my neck. It meant a sleepless night. I spent from 11 p.m. until 2:30 a.m. in the ER. I returned home and couldn't sleep until 5 a.m. I was alone that night. I had to drive myself there and back, a fact that would become relevant. I spent the day tired. In pain, unable to get any meaningful nutrition down, I was still exhausted as this third night came around.

On the third night, I awoke and spat something out from the back of my throat. My fears were confirmed; it's fresh blood. I'm bleeding in the back of my throat—nothing on my lips or tongue. I spat a few more times, still bleeding. I'm terrified. I should go to the ER immediately. The bleeding wasn't stopping. I am so tired. I can't make the same drive I did the night before. It's a five-minute drive in the middle of the night. I have hardly slept in 48 hours. I've been pushing myself. I can push myself. In my younger days, it was physical things like farming and sports. A coach called me "Nails" because, despite my stature, he said I was as tough as nails. As an adult, instead of pushing my body to be healthy, I pushed myself to be the best physician I could be to every person God put in front of me.

At this moment, I am out of gas, completely exhausted. It's 4 a.m. I'm alone in my apartment. All the willpower in the world wouldn't get my body to be able to drive. I am like a team late in the fourth quarter that has left it all out on the field. I've marched down the field, grinding it out for days. Now it's fourth and long, and my body is done. The sweat, blood, and tears emptied onto the field wasn't enough. I am not moving this ball further, at least not by myself. My body (the player) is done, but my mind (the coach) isn't.

I have two plays I can call. The most logical—call 911 to take me to the ER, or a second crazy play—I lean into Jesus. Lean in like I never have before. I put faith in God to get the first down I need, to stop this bleeding, and keep my game of life alive. I am so weak that I need him to carry me, like "footprints in the sand." Weak and scared, I do something crazy. Something that is not like me in a medical emergency situation.

In desperation, I turn to prayer and hand the ball to Jesus. Don't you want the ball in his hands when your game is on the line? Doing something like this at a critical point in my life took strong faith and complete exhaustion. I have nothing left to give. It's an intersection of faith and weakness. A weak body but a willing spirit. This faith I didn't have five years ago. I didn't have it until I started to read scripture. This scripture is written in my heart. I needed the lessons and prayers I learned in Church. Church, for most of my life, had previously been a few times a year thing, a responsibility to check a box. For the past five years, Church has been central to my life. Increasing my time with Jesus in these ways allowed me, in my weakest moments, to access scripture, prayers, and songs as easily as I do my name. Bleeding and exhausted, I need every prayer, verse, and song weaved into my mind, body, and soul in the past five years.

I believed in Jesus as a historical figure in my younger days. He died for our sins, loved us, and was sent from heaven. I didn't believe he was still actively doing miracles today. My faith muscle trained over the five years. Now I believe in the power of an almighty to do miracles right here and now in my apartment. Instead of calling 911, I desperately pray that God stops this bleeding.

You might say this was a dumb decision. It was in faith but also out of exhaustion. Even calling 911 means I must be awake for an ambulance ride. I don't think I can even stay awake for that. I know I will probably fall asleep immediately after this prayer. Faith and science are my guiding principles, so I also set the alarm for 10 minutes. I am not testing God. I believe faith must be coupled with action. I could fall asleep and still be bleeding. Praying, I also place myself in a "safe position," I lean forward and to the side on my couch. I wrap pillows around me and set myself so that any blood will hopefully come out and forward. I'm calling on my savior, but 911 is next. I am scared, tired, and feeling hopeless. I pray, as I close my eyes. If that alarm goes off and I'm still bleeding, I'm calling 911. The bleeding becomes worse? I'm calling 911. If I start coughing? I'm calling 911. Shortness of breath? I'm calling... Ghostbusters. No, I am just checking to see if you are paying attention. It's ten minutes till 911.

One minute goes by; I spit up blood. For two or three more minutes, I spit blood again and again. I pray again, begging God to stop this bleeding. I'm thinking about the woman whose bleeding stopped when she touched Jesus. Jesus explained she was healed by strong faith. I'm hoping my faith is that strong. It feels stronger than ever. I believe he's already stopped my bleeding once two nights ago. I'm seven minutes away from calling 911 though. Believing in the power of prayer but understanding there is a science to medicine that I must respect. Jesus says to keep knocking at the door. I am knocking again with another prayer. Science, I understand. The complexity of prayers though, I don't fully understand. I defer to wiser people with more training than me. I will share a few thoughts related to my reflection on this night.

Taking a break from the bleeding guy on the couch for a minute. Prayers are different from on-demand TV. On-demand TV plays a movie when I ask it to, without thinking. I'm asking God to do something. I communicate with God via prayer. I communicate with my TV via a remote. Both know what I want and when I want it done. There's a difference, though. My TV is under my control, on demand. God is not like that. I don't get to call him and tell him what to do. You can't buy him at a store. There is no upgrade to a newer version in a few years as part of a Black Friday sale. Can you imagine the line at the local supestore for that one? "Half off the new Big Screen God, now with on-demand prayer and sin rewind buttons."

To continue our analogy, if I ask the TV and God to grant my wishes, one serves me. One loves me. God is a loving God who forgives and wants the best for us. God can work miracles. It doesn't mean he's going to tonight. What's different though, is unlike my TV God loves with more wisdom than I fully understand. Sometimes there's a reason prayer goes unanswered. Sometimes it's because what we think we want isn't what's best for us.

For example, if I have an interview in the morning, I should get some sleep but instead I order an "on-demand" movie or decide to binge watch a series. The TV serves me, but doesn't love me. It plays that movie at midnight, answering my request, not caring whether it's a good request. God is different; he loves but doesn't serve me. In love, he often answers requests; other times in infinite wisdom he knows I shouldn't get my way. He doesn't let me watch that movie. He knows I need sleep. Earthly parents love their children. Sometimes we grant requests; at other times we don't because parents understand the big picture. That is the first thing I reflect on about the prayers during this night.

There are other layers. Pastors at my church taught me that sometimes God answers prayers, just not on our timeline. "Not now" doesn't mean "No," just "Not yet." Sometimes people pray for years for things. A delay in answering prayers doesn't mean they won't be. There is a certain beauty in prayers answered years later. Sometimes long-awaited miracles in the waiting can strengthen our faith. We see it through prayer. Wise people pray but also take action. As a physician, I never advise a patient to pray away an addiction or cancer. Still, they can undoubtedly use prayer in a comprehensive program that includes counseling or a biopsy, and specific action items like family support, expert advice, etc. Science and faith complement each other in healing; they don't oppose each other unless we decide to use only one exclusively.

Back to the addiction battle. Some people heal the first time they decide to try to get sober. When it works, it is easy to wonder whether prayer, personal willpower, a good rehab program, or all of the above achieved it.

On the contrary, what happens when it has been decades? When someone's family member struggles with sobriety for years. Every earthly option fails, but the family keeps praying. They might feel it's pointless and wonder why God isn't answering. Then decades into a struggle, they see an answered prayer. It shows God was listening. He answered in love, just not "on demand." In those cases, the beauty lies in the clarity of what and "who" did it. We need to combine prayer with action; sometimes it is pure prayer, and sometimes both. There are entire sermons on when, how, and why prayers go unanswered. I defer to more knowledgeable people if you still have questions. I am an old farm boy simply sharing my faith journey.

I take heart in a few things. First, God loves us so much that he sent his only son to earth, who shed his blood just to prove that love is real, and who sees the entire world as a chessboard and knows what else is coming. With love for all the pieces he moves them in unison to accomplish a greater good for all. He turns what our enemy meant for evil into good. So, we should pray but also realize that there are things we don't know or can't understand at the moment. Twice in my life cancer called "check" on me, whilst moving into the "kill position," yet another piece on the board was moved just in time to save me. Science, yes, but also faith. People of tremendous scientific skill and human empathy; some doctors, some friends, others family, regardless of title or personal relationship to me are all known individually by Jesus. Jesus loves all the pieces on the board equally—the pawns, knights, the Queen and King are all loved. I am a piece meant to turn and serve others. At times I pray for myself; other times, for people I know; other times, for strangers.

To that point, I am returning to myself on the couch that night of July 31. I am lying there in one of the weakest moments of my life, praying for God to stop this bleeding. I can only tell my version of events. I know others had also prayed for me in this battle.

It may be my prayers that night, or others from weeks earlier that matter. I came to the five-minute mark. I feel that sensation in the back of my throat; I spat. Another napkin turns red. I'm discouraged. I will likely end up in the OR. I should get off this couch. I'm exhausted; it hurts to keep my eyes open. I return to leaning forward and pray again—five minutes left on the alarm. In a fog, I wonder if I should press 911. Just get the process started, except I hear the aforementioned alarm. Five minutes were left the last time I looked, but as I feared, I fell asleep.

Here it is, I spat again, knowing it was too dangerous to wait. It's clear! I spit again, still clear. I wish I could tell you I jumped for joy. Like in the movies, the fans go wild at a "miracle" touchdown. That's what's supposed to be right, except this isn't some made-up story. It was my real-life miracle that night. No one else is here to carry me off the football field cheering. I simply remember thinking the bleeding has stopped. I wanted to sleep so badly. Exhausted, I did fall asleep, believing it was divine intervention and praying that God would awaken me if I bleed again. In the biggest gamble of my life, I decide I am going to sleep and not set another alarm; I need to rest. In my weakest moment in this game of life, I just got a miracle pass. Jesus, on fourth-and-long, got me a fresh set of downs to play with. I am using this first down to rest my body. Too tired to think, I sleep.

What I didn't realize though, was at that moment I had just lived a Bible verse I had sent to countless people. I am not the type to minimize medical risk; one would expect me to have called 911. I was wondering why on Earth I hadn't. At no other time have I simply put so much into my faith and so little into my medical training. I wouldn't advise only faith healing without science. Why did I act differently this time, and why was this prayer answered? Then that verse, one of my favorites hit me. Mathew 11: 28-30 was as real as it gets. *"Come to me, all who labor and are heavy laden, and I will give you rest. [29] Take my yoke upon you, and learn from me; for I am gentle and lowly in heart, and you will find rest for your souls. [30] For my yoke is easy, and my burden is light."*

Jesus knew I needed rest that night. I had labored through days of weight loss, pain, and lack of sleep, with my last 72 hours having dealt me a devastating blow. Like a loving parent tucking a child in after a long day, this wasn't so much about stopping bleeding that night as it was about providing rest. I needed that night more than ever. His yoke gave me rest. A yoke is used so two oxen can share a load most of the time. A yoke does allow one oxen to rest IF it is willing to continue to walk alongside the other oxen, and that other oxen is willing to pull even harder for a little while. Yoked to Jesus, he did the heavy lifting. I just had to walk with him.

I'm amazed at the power of our God and my stupidity. Both are impressive. A lot of my friends and family are also amazed by my foolishness. Hours later when I woke up, I laughed. As noted just before going to sleep, I prayed, "In case you didn't do that can you wake me up if I bleed again." In my relationship with Christ as a humble sinner, I often imagine Jesus shaking his head at me. This had to be one of those times. He just saved me twice over three nights, yet here I am saying, God, you probably answered a prayer. You probably got this, but just one last thing, don't forget to wake me if I bleed. I see Jesus beside the Father, looking down and saying, "Go to sleep you bonehead, I got this," shaking his head, "Really, Neal, you aren't sure that was me. It was 4 a.m. in your apartment. You were the only one there and fell asleep on the job! Who do you think it was?" I suspect a few times a week, Jesus in love, half laughing and half frustrated, looks down at me and shakes his head over the mistakes I made and lessons misunderstood. He loves me and knows I am trying, but I probably drive him nuts sometimes.

It may not be an image you have of Jesus; that's ok. Jesus loves EACH of us individually. It is a deep and personal love. I think there is the Jesus we all know, certain fundamental truths if you will. He also does a few things, so we know he knows us personally. I share what he did for me that night, but it wasn't necessarily MY PRAYER that was answered; I had a prayer team. Many friends and family prayed. They were also praying or had prayed in advance for me. It was all of us together. I thank them. I want them to know God heard each of them. They must know he also answered our prayers that night. Jesus didn't just do this for me; he also did it for them. They said, "Jesus, win one for the Gipper," that night. I was the Gipper, but they may be the Gipper next time!

I want to end this by returning to the point that modern medicine and science are critically important healing aspects; prayer is also key, and can be combined. ONLY praying and ignoring good science is not wise. Sometimes God uses a doctor, nurse, or therapist in our healing. Retelling my cancer journey would be incomplete without acknowledging the intertwined roles of science and faith. That bloodstained shirt with "Jesus Saves" will never be washed again; it is framed as a reminder of both.

Chapter 4

The Patient and Crumble Cookies.

One difficult thing about going through cancer when you are a parent of a child under 18 is that you find yourself simultaneously in the role of a caregiver but also needing to be cared for. Your caregiving is, in part, limited by your own health needs.

It's humbling. My first time going through cancer in 2017, my radiation oncologist described me as a beast. It was the fastest he had seen anyone ever come off the narcotic pain medicine. There was a reason for that. Getting off scheduled narcotic pain medicines as fast as possible was emotionally important. I knew as long as I was on them I could not fully, without assistance, be responsible for my daughter's basic needs. I wasn't going to drive her anyplace while taking narcotics. Plus, narcotic medicines can make one sleepy. I felt it best to have another adult around us when I had her during these times.

I also needed to arrange for other people to help with transport. There were many people that assisted us. I'm grateful for all the friends and family that stepped up to help. It didn't change the fact that I partially felt incomplete as a parent. Until you've been through it, it's hard to know and describe what it's like. When you're a parent with a medical condition and you can't provide the most basic needs for your child without the help of others, it's hard. I didn't feel whole until I had taken back this responsibility. Being a dad is the greatest job I will ever have, and it's a far more critical role than any paycheck-driven job I have ever had. Even a few weeks of a limited capacity like this was hard, but not because of pride or an unwillingness to accept help. I was accepting help. It was sad to know my daughter was also going through this. So yes, there's a parenting part for which I have a goal to accomplish—getting off narcotic pain medicine as fast as possible.

Maybe you don't have cancer, but is something interfering with your ability to parent to the best of your ability? Is that gambling or porn addiction taking time away from your kids? Does being hungover on a Saturday make you less interactive with them? Is the money you spend on hotel rooms or flowers for someone you shouldn't be with taking away from their college fund? Hopefully, my story of wanting to get off pain medications can help heal a family hurting from these things. There was a trade-off here for me, and there will be for you. I accepted the physical pain being higher than I would have liked to parent how I would like. You, too, may have to endure something in the short term you don't want to do.

To a separate group of parents, those permanently disabled, I want to point out that this time was, in some ways, a blessing. I was teaching my daughter to preserve despite obstacles. So to the parent who uses a wheelchair, keep showing them how never to give up. To the blind parent listening to the audiobook, your child sees your courage. Also, as this next story will illustrate, my illness offered a chance for me to be creative, and in doing so, my daughter and I developed a fun tradition.

Back to our life during the summer and fall of 2022. I want to explain the physical symptoms and how they impacted us.

The pain after a head and neck cancer surgery can be debilitating. Anyone who's had tonsil surgery will tell you it's painful. It makes getting nutrition down challenging. In my situation, I had the tonsil resected and had what's called a lateral neck dissection, where they took out lymph nodes. It's essentially a tonsillectomy plus a second surgery. What a two-for-one sale on OR time, huh? You get two surgeries for the price of one surgical team! Sign me up for that one, right?

During the immediate post-op and later during radiation, it's common for patients to be on multiple pain meds, narcotics being one of them. I still wanted to be a dad and do things for my daughter. We had another adult with us during these times, and I did manage to get in a trip to a bowling alley with my daughter. I couldn't bowl due to surgical issues, but we had fun. I also baked her some of the most delicious cookies in America. Before you ask for my recipe, remember I bake with a credit card. The recipe is to open up your iPhone and grab your wallet. Add credit, allow to mix, and presto! I "baked" and "cooked" some of the most delicious meals you can imagine using plastic and 16 numbers. I had preheated my credit card at a place called Crumble Cookies for delicious gourmet cookies.

These cookies are so delicious you need to get on a treadmill just for reading about them. Download the app. Your doctor will schedule you for a diabetic check in three months. This wasn't about calories, but about my daughter having fun and enjoying something I could provide even when weakened by cancer. With an adult supervising us, off we went to pick up gourmet cookies. Those who know me will tell you that even when I'm not on narcotics, I should probably always have another adult supervising me. Alas, that's an entirely different book as to the reasons why.

My pain was so terrible that the possibility of enjoying a cookie wasn't on my agenda. My mouth and throat hurt terribly. I was losing weight fast. Dietary supplements like Boost and protein shakes provided vitamins and some protein in calories, but not enough calories even when I forced down several a day. The shakes for nutritional supplements came out of my nose to make things even more fun. It makes for a great party trick. Uvula-palatal insufficiency led to all kinds of colored liquids coming out of my nose. I'm like a clown with a disgusting party trick? Pick your favorite color and hand me that strawberry Boost and watch this!

Getting a spoon with applesauce or yogurt in my mouth without intense pain is difficult. I've never cried from physical pain, but there were moments I was close to it. With head and neck cancer, you have two stretches where you are dealing with this pain; the first after surgery, then again after radiation. It's not uncommon for people to need a feeding tube. I was able to avoid a feeding tube thanks to new science, AND well, I have just enough of a "dad bod" that I had enough calories saved up in my midsection. I planned all those years ago and packed on a few pounds in case I got cancer. Or at least that's my story, and I'm sticking to it. So she and my friend enjoy the cookies; we even created a "rating system" where they judged each flavor.

I discovered a method to consume additional calories by directly applying frosting to my tongue, bypassing the need to chew or swallow. Over 48 hours,

I consumed a crumbled cookie, allowing frosting and cookie fragments to dissolve in my mouth. This realization might be surprising, but cookies contain a significant sugar content that can readily dissolve. Shocking!

Cookies are proof that God loves us and wants us to be happy, I guess. I stole that from Ben Franklin, who may or may not have said, "Beer is proof God loves us and wants to be happy." Hold on before you go out to get a 12-pack (I am looking at you, Wisconsin, yes, you! Your baseball team is named the Brewers, and the mascot slides into a beer mug). God sends us all kinds of things as proof he wants us to be happy. Our creator hardwired into millions of us the enjoyment of laughter, sunsets, rainbows, a baby's smile, and music. These things have touched the hearts of millions of people over the generations. Traditions of music are passed on over time.

The tradition of crumble cookies my daughter and I started when I couldn't eat them. Now we make fun memories by checking the flavors each week. We discuss money and health, deciding if that week's flavors are worth the calories or money. We score them on a 1-10 scale when we try each flavor. We talk about tipping the employees and being kind to servers. I hope for years to come, crumble or some gourmet cookie will remind her of my sweet love for her. In all the hurt, this patient found a way to parent.

Besides cookies, she could see what kindness looked like during this time. She has some of the most amazing "Uber drivers" one could imagine. She was driven around by physicians, farmers, teachers, physical therapists, and vice presidents of banks. Their educational backgrounds, salaries and socioeconomic status sometimes differed, but they all shared a willingness to help their fellow human being in need. Many judge others based on how much money or education they have, the car they drive, the awards they win or the clothes they wear. What truly matters is how you treat others. The beauty of a person doesn't lie in their job title; it lies in their willingness to help their fellow human beings in times of need. Both cancers have been a blessing because they've allowed me to see the true inner beauty of people.

Between 2017 and 2022, that's two post-surgical periods and two post-radiation periods, right side and left side, I experienced stretches of needing pain meds and the Uber armada. That's a total of four stretches where I could only partially parent. I cried in joy when I could come off my narcotic pain medicines. It was a victory.

The moment I looked cancer in the eye and said you can take many things from me; you might take my life, but I'm taking something back on this day. I'm taking back being a parent without help. As the song, *Hard Love* by Needtobreathe[8] says, "I've been trading punches with a heart of darkness," you've landed a couple and knocked me down. These four times, though, I got off the mat and punched back. I showed cancer that it hadn't won yet. I was still in the fight. As parents, we endure suffering of many types to help our children. Parents will go without fancy clothes or a meal so that their kid can attend a camp. Mothers go through the intense pain of childbirth, then sign up to do it again for the next child. Sidenote: women are the superior gender. If God had made it so that males had to give childbirth, the human species would have gone extinct after two generations!

Chapter 5

Parents Preset Radio Stations in the Car

Sometimes we initiate the healing process even before experiencing any hurt. We can start nurturing healing in our children before the world leaves its scars on them.

Let me share a funny story a friend told me about while listening to a popular radio station when a song came on with the line, "staying up all night to get lucky." Their five-year-old child was in the car and asked why someone had to stay up all night to get lucky. The child was thinking about good or bad luck and wondered, "Can't you get lucky during the day?"

Technically, both types of "lucky" can happen at any time, but the child was only aware of one type. The song's adult version of "lucky" was not what the child was referring to. It was a comical parenting moment, and we laughed about it. However, it made me reflect on how radio stations and iPads can introduce concepts to young minds.

I'm not criticizing the song or the parents in this situation. By most standards, the song is benign. One could even argue that the child is lucky to be alive because their parents did indeed get lucky one night. Or maybe it was during the day; who knows? I think introducing the idea of staying up all night "to get lucky" to a child while driving to school is worth considering the implications. One song alone doesn't have a significant impact.

However, adding multiple songs with similar themes that kids hear on the radio can start shaping their perception. You might disagree, but can you sing the songs from your teenage years by heart? I bet you can. How about recalling conversations your parents had with you during that time? Which memories occupied your teenage mind when hanging out with friends on weekends without parental supervision? Maybe it was a mix of both, but did they convey slightly different messages?

What if we flipped the switch? What if the songs playing in our cars reinforced the messages we want our kids to hear? Often, we are drawn in by the beats and melodies of the music, paying less attention to the lyrics at first. But there are catchy songs out there with positive lyrics. Why would advertising agencies spend so much on theme songs if lyrics didn't matter? Can you complete the jingles for "Nationwide is on..." or "You save big money at..." or "The best part of waking up is...?" I believe lyrics do matter, at least to some extent. I might be wrong, but what harm is there in listening to positive ones?

Both positive and negative songs can have catchy tunes. When I started listening to songs from a parent's perspective, I realized that some songs I considered "fun" had lines I didn't necessarily support. So, when my daughter was in the car, I started playing radio stations and artists with positive lyrics. When she wasn't with me, I would switch back to the stations I enjoyed, ranging from top 40 hits to country, classic rock, and NPR. Without realizing it, those positive lyrics when my daughter was in the car also positively impacted me. I was drawn to songs with positive lyrics even when she wasn't around. The music became enjoyable and part of my healing journey, inspiring me to be kinder, more empathetic, and more dedicated to making the world a better place. We started sharing songs we liked back and forth.

As my daughter grows, she is still a few years away from dating and experiencing nights without her parents. However, it brings me great comfort to know that she was exposed to music that prepares her for these future situations with a positive message. Songs such as *Before You Ask Her* by Matthew West[9]. These songs align with the values we teach her and reinforce them. It's important to recognize that different parents have varying perspectives on what they consider positive or negative lyrics. I'm not here to impose my definition of positive lyrics on you. Instead, I emphasize that the music we cherish, with its captivating beats, can be accompanied by positive, neutral, or negative lyrics. And if lyrics matter, why not leverage them to support the message we want to convey?

I realized this through the experience of a friend's son. Sometimes it takes time to discover artists, radio stations, and songs that consistently offer uplifting lyrics and delightful beats. We live in a remarkable era where we can create personalized playlists on our phones. I curate my own playlists because some songs may not receive airtime.

I may be mistaken, but even a broken clock is right twice a day, and even a blind squirrel finds a nut. So, why not take the opportunity to prove me wrong? Embrace the power of music to influence our lives and our children's lives positively.

Chapter 6

Parenting with Athletes, YouTubers, and Speakers

Most of my childhood heroes were athletes, but for kids today, heroes can be singers, athletes, actresses, influencers, and more. Initially, athletes became my heroes simply because I saw them on TV or in person. I looked up to them before knowing much about their characters. Unfortunately, some of them went on to commit terrible deeds, which were easy to reject as wrong. Others engaged in slightly questionable behavior, leading me to believe those actions were acceptable because my heroes did them. To a certain extent, our children's interests and exposure play a significant role in determining their heroes. Parents learning more about the athletes, actors, or YouTubers our children admire allows us to highlight their positive contributions while discussing instances that present learning opportunities. Sometimes the kid's hero's behavior may not have been ideal. Good people make mistakes, just as bad people can occasionally do good things. Parents are busy and can't know everything, but even researching a few celebrities creates a discussion.

Beyond our children's interests, we can expose them to positive speakers and actors by selecting uplifting content for ourselves. Every week, my daughter and I listen to a speaker from an organization whose mission and values align with ours. This organization generously donates money and promotes activities to assist people in third-world countries. They also support individuals in the U.S. dealing with divorce and addiction, amongst other things. The speakers we listen to are funny, humble, and kind, compassionately delivering messages aiming to make the world a better place.

During these talks, we share laughter and find healing. My daughter gains strength that will help her navigate adversity in life. I had the opportunity to meet one of these speakers, and when my daughter heard about it, her face lit up. She expressed her desire to meet that person as well. When he graciously agreed to meet her, I realized he had become one of her first heroes in life. This hero, like any other, is not perfect. Like me, he has flaws. Although I may not agree with everything he says, the 98% I do agree with earns him the privilege of still being listened to, despite our slight differences in perspective. He is the kind of person I want to teach my daughter about treating others and facing life's challenges. I reinforce positivity by dedicating a little time each week to these messages.

I cannot determine who my daughter will choose as her heroes. However, I can provide her diverse role models beyond athletes and YouTubers. I can offer feedback on heroes when I observe them doing positive or negative things. We engage in conversations about why people may behave in certain ways and discuss their actions' potential positive or negative consequences. We also engage in healthy disagreements, even if we largely agree with them but have different perspectives on one or two issues. It's like that favorite radio station of yours—if they play one bad song, do you reject it? No, you trust that the next one will be good.

As a doctor and patient, I have experienced starting medications in both roles. Sometimes one medication causes unpleasant side effects, but it doesn't mean I give up on medication entirely. I simply switch to a different one. Radio stations, medications, counselors, and speakers can all have flaws, but that doesn't mean we should give up on music, science, therapy, or podcasts. I often tell my patients, "If counseling didn't work, it's okay to give up on the counselor, but don't give up on counseling." If a hero disappoints you, it doesn't mean every hero will disappoint you. If a church in the past failed you I'm sorry, but I hope you would consider trying a new church in the future. I started going back to church in my late 30's and it changed my life.

My daughter found a hero in our church pastor, and it made me realize the importance of finding individuals or organizations whose views align with ours. Consider incorporating occasional messages from such speakers or organizations into your children's lives, even if it's just a few times a month. This allows you to introduce someone who reinforces your shared values and expresses ideas in a way that resonates with your kids. In the worst-case scenario, you spend quality time with your child while listening to a speaker you enjoy.

I have also found inspiration from individuals outside the church, including former presidents, governors, inspirational speakers, and authors. These people come from diverse backgrounds and have different views and life experiences. When connecting with them, my criteria isn't based on their similarity to me or complete agreement with my beliefs. Instead, I look for individuals who demonstrate a good heart, deliver predominantly positive messages, and make me think. That's enough for me.

One final thought on speakers: personal growth also happens when we listen to people we disagree with. It's possible to find wisdom in what they say, even if we disagree fully. Similarly, when we listen to people we agree with, we should remain open to identifying aspects of their message that may not be optimal. Recognizing both the good and the less favorable aspects of a message, regardless of our opinion of the speaker, indicates active processing and listening. Unfortunately, we often focus too much on the messenger, preventing us from critically analyzing the message and instead resorting to complete agreement or disagreement with everything said.

Chapter 7

Physician: Heal Yourself
Before You Hurt

Hope for the best, but prepare for the worst. I have shared this with countless patients and families as a physician. Usually in uncertain times for them, where medically things could go badly, all hope isn't lost. A humble honor of my job has been being able to walk with and counsel people during some of their scariest moments in life. As a physician, I play a dual role in making the objective medical decision to try to save lives and heal. Starting antibiotics in the ICU, IV drips of blood thinners, trying to take fluid off to help a stressed heart. These are a few of the "levers" I pull up or down to ride the wave and get people's bodies through dangerous storms. There is also the subjective, compassionate part of having conversations with patients and families. The soul of medicine is where empathy is needed to listen to what matters to people—giving realistic perspective on what COULD happen in the best and worst case scenarios, and what is MOST LIKELY. Most things in medicine aren't 100% certain.

One thing that is 100% is that we all face adversity—health, relationship, financial, spiritual, and social can take countless forms. A great way to heal yourself is to live where you "hope for the best, prepare for the worst." A storm of some sort is coming; it's in your future. We don't know when or what, but we will all face something. I've been through a few rodeos of them in my life: cancer twice, a divorce, stressful career situations, living poor, etc. We all have gone through things. In no way is my life harder than the next person's. If you're reading this, I do not doubt you also have scars, things I can't imagine that would make a person's blood boil. I hope our past hurts can be healed, but I also hope we can start healing even before the next hurt comes our way.

This next part is about our future battles; preparing us and our families for them. You can start healing even before you're hurting. Just like a team prepares for a game before they play, or a general trains soldiers before a battle. A coach prepares his or her team for battle. He coaches his players. She has the team practice the play not once or twice, but several times. They know that preparation beforehand is key. They comfort themselves saying, "this is what you train for." Knowing you are prepared gives one peace of mind when a disaster strikes. I am reminded of John 16: 33 *"I have told you these things, so that in me you may have peace. In this world you will have trouble. But take heart! I have overcome the world"*

Your future hurts, maybe a sudden loss of a loved one, but you can start healing before they die by telling them you love them, you're sorry, and you forgive them. Your future hurt may come in the form of an unfair termination from work. You can start healing in advance if you make budget decisions that allow you a less expensive lifestyle. Maybe you wait one more year on that new car or do one less vacation this year. Maybe it will be an unexpected request by the person you love to be together no longer. You can pre-heal if you are establishing a healthy, supportive relationship now. Maybe you don't have many friends, but who knows what may come from volunteering or joining a small group. Taking these steps accomplishes two things: first, there is the concrete objective of having some savings, a good friend to lean on, or that you are already at peace with your efforts to heal a strained relationship. Second, an intangible emotional peace comes from knowing you are prepared for this. You got this. As Jackie Robinson said, "This ain't fun, but you watch me, I'll get it done." The preparation I did in life BEFORE the hurt of the scalpel or the pain of my relationship ending meant at least some of the healing had already started.

Case in point, back to John 16: 1, *"I have told you these things so you won't abandon your faith."* Battles are often lost because people lose faith; discipline breaks down, desperation sets in, panic takes over, the amygdala kicks in, and the frontal lobe's thoughtful plan falls apart. No army can win a battle if soldiers get scared and run away. Not remembering what you are taught when you are in a battle of any kind is a recipe for disaster. Soldiers need discipline in battle, surgeons need to trust their training when complications arise, and teachers need their frontal lobes in a classroom of screaming kids to practice healthy techniques. Teams need to run the play the same way when they are down by three, inbounding the basketball with four seconds left in the championship game the same way they do it in practice. In difficult moments it's important not to abandon what you were taught.

Several years ago, my dad and I had a strained relationship. However, I am incredibly thankful we took steps to heal our bond. I would like to share this journey of pre-hurt healing with you.

We both could point to things the other one had done, and truth be told; we were both in the wrong to a degree. We were both right to a degree. We were both stubborn and dug into our positions. Thankfully though, a few years back, we started to take steps to at least forgive one another and admit we weren't perfect. Slowly, the relationship healed with us both taking positive action. It had been back to normal and healthier than ever two years before I was diagnosed with cancer in 2022. That was a blessing in so many ways. Emotionally I didn't have to worry about dying without making amends with him. Logistically he was there to help me when I had a drain hanging out of my neck and had to try to shower. Trust me, when you'll have to let someone see you naked, the list of people you're comfortable with doing that is pretty short. It's not the kind of thing you ask a coworker to do. I had lots of emotions to process, but thankfully I had "pre-checked" being at peace with the status of my relationship with my dad, which is great because I can make fun of him later in this book!

Next, on my journey of pre-healing, I sought counseling to address the stress and anxiety I was facing. While I may not have direct experience with all the topics discussed in this book, I have battled with depression and anxiety. I believe sharing my insights can be valuable. The counseling helped me see the world and people differently and understand how to better be at peace with things. This pre-healed some of the mental hurt around cancer. Also, for me, a huge part was in the years before this second cancer appeared. I had grown my faith from it being a few times a year at Sunday service, to something that was an anchor in my life during the storm of cancer. By having a savings account, I had some of my medical bills prepaid, which also helped. Given my current job I realize it's easier to save, but I will point out that even when I was a poor farm kid mowing lawns in college, I still saved. My savings sometimes were small. I sometimes had only $20, but I've lived life trying to be ready for the next rainy day.

If you're reading this and life seems good, I am so happy for you. I hope it stays that way for a long time. Let's hope for the best but prepare for the worst. So look at life like a storm is coming, and see what parts you want to reinforce. When a storm hits, floodwaters rise fast. Start grabbing sandbags to pre-heal. Reinforce your finances, faith, relationships, and physical or mental health today, so that you have the resources you need when you go into battle. After all, "Momma always said there would be days like these."

My daughter and I had no idea we would face cancer in the summer of 2022, yet we were preparing, so prepared that a nine-year-old had a Bible verse and a prayer her Senior Pastor taught her at church. She knew what to tell Dad that morning of surgery when she repeated a prayer learned months earlier. "Holy Spirit, fill me with your strength," and I repeated it when I was alone at 4 a.m. on the couch that night 12 days later.

We didn't just share prayers; we shared songs. One we love is Anne Wilson's song, *Sunday Sermons*.[15] "Those roots run deep… No matter what the world throws at me, I know His word is true… I could hear my savior telling me how much He loves me…."

That last part, the savior calling me. I love that her savior, your savior, my savior, our savior, NEVER stops calling us.

Chapter 8

Patient: Why We Choose Not to Heal

I consider myself an empathic person, some consider me a stupid person, maybe both are correct? I have an abundance of empathy, sometimes to an overwhelming extent. When social injustice occurs, when someone discriminates, when the truth twists or when someone experiences physical or emotional pain, I can't help but share their pain. I share a mixture of anger, sadness, and frustration with them. We often find ourselves clinging to anger, even knowing that it harms us. But why do we stay in that state?

One reason is that we may mistakenly believe we are taking action in our anger. We may think that by being angry on someone else's behalf, we are somehow helping to heal their wounds. However, does our anger truly provide any solace or aid to them? It can have the opposite effect. Let's consider a scenario in football: a player is hit after the play. Witnessing this, his teammate becomes angry and retaliates by shoving the opposing player. If you're a football fan, you know the second player involved in such situations is given the penalty. Announcers often say, "It's the second guy who gets the flag." The referee didn't see the initial offense, but they witnessed how anger provoked the second player's response. As a result, not only did the original player get unfairly hit but there is now a penalty against his team. The justified anger of his teammate ultimately made the situation worse for both of them.

There is an analogy here with incidents such as school shootings. Over the past 20-plus years, we have witnessed a worsening of this situation. During my high school experience, such events were unheard of and extremely rare. We never practiced active shooter scenarios back then, but now schools invest significant time and resources in them. While most people agree that there are measures we can take, we may differ in our opinions on the specific extent of those measures. However, we have become so consumed by anger towards

Republicans or Democrats that we inadvertently reward a system that thrives on our resentment toward anyone who doesn't align perfectly with our views.

What happens when our anger prevents us from considering even one or two propositions the opposite party offers? More children fall victim to shootings, more families suffer, and more people are hurt because we are too distracted by our rage to address the multiple root causes. Use the past 20 years as evidence to support this point—it's only getting worse, yet none of us want it to. I am not taking a political stance on any particular law or approach, nor am I endorsing or opposing any party here. I am simply making an observation.

Psalm 37: 8. "*Stop being angry, turn away from your rage. Do not lose your temper, it only leads to harm*" Maybe the most underrated verse in the Old Testament. Think about that, what if that football player didn't retaliate? What if those politicians and neighbors didn't lose their tempers but worked out a few reasonable compromises? There would be less harm if we didn't turn to anger. Instead, in each situation, things got worse for the team and for the country.

"You catch more flies with sugar than with vinegar." No one likes to be insulted or have their faults pointed out. So when we put vinegar out to the opposition, it doesn't get far. It might make you feel good or justified, but laws don't get passed. Work promotions don't happen, marriages don't heal, and teams end up in third and long from the penalty you got for helping your teammate. If, instead, you find one simple thing to complement that difficult coworker, one thing you share in common with that family member from the opposite party, and hand them some honey instead, guess what might happen? You might get some honey back, and you both win. Throwing vinegar at them will likely have it thrown back at you.

Why might someone decide to keep drinking even after accepting that it's hurting people they care about, including themselves? It's a short-term fix to "numb the pain or stress" of a difficult situation. The healthy healing is more demanding than the immediate albeit temporary "healing" a hit or 12-pack provides.

Other physiological, genetic, and social factors are at play, but I call this out for these reasons. The alcoholic who already feels bad when you tell them you are done with them until they get clean, adds to the social isolation. You add to the guilt, and they want that short-term unhealthy healing. I am not saying we should stay in unhealthy relationships; we often must distance ourselves. However, we can do so with love and by pointing them in the right direction if we at least understand it's not a personal failure that they relapsed. Sometimes it's a hurt they need to heal in a healthier way, which may or may not be with us in their life. These situations require experts and vary greatly on a case-to-case basis, so please don't use this paragraph to decide what to do.

Sometimes ironically, people don't want to heal. In high school and college, I worked a job that required me to be covered in dirt, grass, and grimy clothes. When I would go out in public, I liked that people who saw me in that state would know I was a hard worker. I bought myself a car and paid $300; it was worth every penny, not more. It was rusted, the window didn't roll down, it was loud, and sometimes when you turned the key off the engine would keep running for another minute. It was kind of a piece of sh... More on that later. However, I loved driving the thing because anyone who saw me would know I paid for it. It was the kind of car only a poor kid who paid for it with his own money would drive. What does this have to do with not wanting to heal? Simply, these badges of honor were a part of my identity. A nicer car or a less demanding job would have made my life easier. But I didn't want things to be easy because I was proud of what I did to earn my paycheck or scar. Sometimes pride prevents us from improving our situation because in a stubborn way, we want to "prove we can do it," so we turn down the help of a neighbor when we are widowed and raising children. We don't want surgery to heal that aching knee because we want to prove we can fight the pain. Living life as a "lone wolf" and keeping people at a distance proves you survived the past rejections or abuse of others, and you don't "need" anyone.

Let me flip the perspective if this is you or someone you know. Maybe it's not about what WE CAN ENDURE; perhaps it's about what healing others can and want to give us. Maybe in your pride, you are being selfish and not thinking about how good it would make the neighbor feel to help you. Maybe they already admire you for your strength, so stop proving yourself and let them show you what they can do. Maybe the real courage isn't in being a "lone wolf" survivor, but in defeating those who hurt you by healing yourself enough so you can love and be loved again.

If you were hungry and someone made you a delicious meal and put it in front of you, would there be "honor" in saying I will not eat your food? I want to prove how I can endure hunger, so you see how strong I am. Or would you be insulting the cook? Try that trick the next time your mother-in-law invites you over for Easter. Let me know how it goes. "Oh, it's ok; I am showing my strength to endure hunger." You might want to throw a pillow on the couch, as there is a good chance you will sleep on it!

While you're at it, get that knee looked at so my surgical friend can pay me back the $10 they owe me; otherwise I will name them in my next book. It's been over two years! Every surgeon thinks, "Did I forget to pay Neal back?" If you're not sure, send me $10 anyways!

Understanding why someone doesn't want to be healed allows us to reframe our conversations when we try to encourage them to get the care or the help others want to offer. It requires empathy and listening. There is a powerful way to change your dynamic completely; instead of telling them they should get help, ask them, "What concerns do you have about…?" I am amazed at how much more effective I am with people who aren't complying with treatment, when instead of telling them the good and bad things if they don't, I simply ask, "What concerns do you have?" When you listen to someone, even if you may not agree 100% with their rationale, it shows them they matter; their opinion counts, their pain is heard, and you want to understand them. When you tell them what they should do or why they should do it, you project superiority over them. It can sound like you think you are better than them. This doesn't just apply to physical healing. If you want to make progress on a project with a difficult person at work, see what happens when you change from arguing your point to listening to theirs. "What are your thoughts on? Can I get your opinion about…? Have you considered this?" Asking questions gives you insight you may not have, and builds what we call a therapeutic alliance in healthcare. Once you have that, they might ask you a few questions and want your insight. A wise friend taught me this. We all want to know people are for us, not against us. We want to be cheered for and cheer for others.

I am cheering you on in whatever your current fight is. I wrote this book because we all have battles; we all feel alone, hurt, cry, and wonder why. I am sending the song *Cheering You On* by King and Country[3] to everyone who reads this. I mean it. Life is hard; so many pains. As the song says, we are winning if we choose to love despite it all. If we try one more day, we win. If we defeat anger, we win.

Anger often jumps up out of nowhere; "almost a reflex" is how we respond when something happens out of the blue. However, reflexes are different from behaviors. Not EVERYONE at the game yells at a bad call or lets the other driver know you think they are number one when they cut you off. If it was truly a reflex as a doctor, I should be able to elicit the same response from everyone every time. I have used my reflex hammer on thousands of knees in my career, and each person responds similarly. Not once have I hit someone's knee, and they instantly started doing the Macarena. No, it's predictable and consistent, so predictable that we assume there is a medical problem if we don't get the same response from everyone. Sidenote, if you want to make your doctor's day plan ahead; get ready for when they hit your knee and after the reflex, start doing the Macarena. Do it for 10 seconds, sit down, and say, "Is it odd? That is my reflex!"

Why did I use the Macarena prank to talk about reflexes and anger? Let's summarize. Reflexes aren't modifiable, but behavior is. Anger is an emotion not a reflex, and it only gets to drive behavior if you let it pounce in an instant, but you can control it. To pull off that prank, you will have to practice the dance, and you are assuming the doctor will check reflexes. We can also plan for those moments of anger; we can assume they will come around. You may need to practice, and sometimes you won't get it right. Controlling my anger, I have been practicing for the past four years and it's still a work in progress. Lastly, you are going to need help. Help from others, maybe a professional counselor, a spouse, or perhaps a close friend you admire for their ability to stay cool, calm, and collected. Or conceivably from someone who used to be hot-tempered, but you noted a change. What do they do differently now? It might be exercising, more sleep, meditation, and possibly from scripture or songs about love, peace, and kindness that have just as uplifting tunes in the background as the lyrics as those about sex, violence, and hate. Miraculous changes sometimes happen slowly by taking one simple step.

Chapter 9

Physician: What We Can't Afford

A friend was dealing with a troublesome unethical employee. Given short staffing, my friend claimed, "I can't afford to let them go."

My reply was, "You can't afford to keep them." They will create bigger problems if you do. Changing and giving up something in the short term is scary. We only think about what we will lose and the short-term hardship. Set that alarm an hour early to workout? We think about the sleep we'll lose, forgetting about the extra energy we will have long-term if we start to workout. Take a few weeks from work to address a mental health or addiction issue. We think about the short-term loss of finances. Not realizing the mental health or addiction might cost you your job in 6 months if you don't address it now. We don't realize we will get a promotion two years from now because addressing that issue makes us better employees.

Are you admitting that you gambled again, are having an affair, or stolen money from work? You fear this may mean the loss of a marriage or the respect of family and friends; it will come out eventually. You might be in a bad situation but don't make it worse. If you are the one to admit it instead of being "caught," you are in a better position to save your marriage, job, or friendships. Marriages are sometimes saved when people reflect on why they are in the crisis and work to change it. This applies to safe marriages. Abusive relationships aren't safe places for healing together.

The abusive partner controls the finances, and you have no job? You may meet someone at the women's shelter who sees talent in you that you don't see in yourself. A new career awaits. Are you staying to protect the kids? Could it be teaching them either to be an abuser or to stay with an abuser? Will the abuser hurt them more? I know you're scared, but no one deserves abuse. People want to help you; give them that chance. You may think you can't afford to leave, but maybe you can't afford to stay.

I feared moving from being a casual believer in Jesus to becoming a follower. Going to church a few times a year was enough. I didn't need to change. I didn't want to "give up" having fun. Speaking of exercise, in college I used to be up till 4 a.m. "exercising" my liver on the weekend; three dollars for a cup and the cheapest beer in all the land was yours. I made a large return on investment! The "bible thumper" Christians in college were simply not having as much fun as I was, or so I thought. I knew some of them; they were nice, but spending Friday nights in a dorm instead of a house party or attending a bible study instead of the football game on Saturday was not for me! Now in my 40s, I lead a bible study with a hilarious group of people. I sometimes start it with, "WAZ UP, MY SINNERS!" This ain't your momma's bible study, and we say, "What happens at bible study stays at bible study." We laugh often.

Reading the bible boring? The Old Testament would be quite the R-rated movie. Voyeurs, cougar's chasing hunky younger men, great battles, affairs, incest, it's all in there. Noah, David, Moses, and Abraham are serious bad boys that make your average Harley rider seem like the PTA president.

Life didn't seem as fun if I started to follow Jesus more, but Galatians 5: 22-23 says. "*Love, joy, peace, patience, goodness, faithfulness, gentleness, and self-control*" were the things inviting the Holy Spirit into my life would produce.

These things (love, joy, patience, etc.) I've been experiencing more over the past few years. Love for more people and greater patience in more situations than previously. I have more understanding of people with different ideological views of the world: politically or theologically. I had joy in my heart even through suffering. The first time I had cancer and the first major relationship that ended, I did not experience joy in either. I was still struggling in the second major relationship that ended, but I started to see how God can show up in our weakest moments. By the time I had cancer for the second time and my third major relationship in life ended, I could still find joy in these difficult times despite the pain. It was weird because I knew how I felt in these same situations previously in my life. This was completely different. I had more peace and calm than I've ever had before. I become emotionally healthier every day.

Self-control sounds like we may be giving up certain things. In reality, we gain things we want but don't have. Self-control prevents damaging words from anger. Self-control over excessive spending gives peace about that unexpected financial burden. Self-control skips being drunk Friday night, so you have more fun with your kids Saturday morning.

Romans 7: 15 *"I don't really understand myself, for I want to do what is right, but I don't. Instead, I do what I hate"*.

Does anyone relate to that; maybe not all the time, but at least on occasion? Having faith, seeing a counselor, working out, and reflecting on my life does not make me better than *anyone* else, but it has made me better than *I* used to. Don't we all want to be a better version of ourselves? If you don't after all, then you're perfect. Just ask your spouse, "Hey honey, I know I am perfect, but would you like me to be more perfect?" It's not just faith that helped me become a better version. There's been counseling, there have been medications, there have been discussions with friends about exercise and there has been better sleep. Faith should be coupled with action. I've learned though, that yes, if you don't have religion, you can certainly get better. There will be people who can point to having used counseling, exercise, self-help books, or meditation and have made significant improvements with an agnostic or atheist worldview. The scientist in me supports these things. You can be a good person and improve yourself with just one of these things. But why only use one prong?

Chapter 10

Physician: Three-pronged Attack

Full healing involves multiple things. Some I've mentioned you may have tried, including counseling, physical therapy, prayer, or meds, but they failed. Does that mean these things didn't work? Your instinct might be to say yes, but let me explain, using a 200-plus-year-old battle plan, and why it did not work.

Was it a one-pronged attack? Or a three-pronged? If you don't remember history class it's ok, I'm a history dork. The three-pronged attack was the British plan that would've won the revolutionary war. A great plan to bring three armies together; it would've wiped out Washington and his homeboys while they were camping. Never heard Washington refer to his army as his homeboys? Again, you should've paid attention in history class; he famously coined the term homeboys. Yeah, in fact, no, I am kidding about the homeboys part, but the rest is true. Three armies were going to meet at Washington at the same time. Kinda like the "meet you at the Quarterback" play defensive linemen like to say when they team up for a sack. Had this three-pronged plan been properly executed, Americans would still be singing God Save the King (or Queen) today.

Here's what happened. One British general thought he could do it alone; three armies seemed excessive. Ladies, doesn't this sound like a typical man? You give them a well-laid plan and half listening they say, "Yeah, yeah, ok. It'll be fine, no big deal, stop worrying. I got this." In fact, for many of you it sounds so familiar you might ask your husband, "By chance, were you a British general in a former life?"

A second army arrived but was weakened by the Minutemen;[16] it didn't arrive exactly at the ideal time or at full strength. So, for practical purposes, Washington only had to fight against one of the three armies. While we all know how that ended; the three-pronged attack was a winning plan, but the one-pronged attack failed. The one army that fought alone (and lost) wasn't the problem. It was the lack of other prongs!

Beautiful plan, execution as ugly as my hair in junior high! In the past, maybe you only used one prong (yoga, meds, or prayer to fight anxiety). Those that failed were not because they were bad ideas but because you needed other prongs. Add counseling for that anxiety and retry one of those three things again. Now you have two prongs. We don't need to limit ourselves to three prongs. I don't know if you are battling physical or emotional pain, trying to lose weight, get into med school, parent a lost teenager, or run a failing company, but I do know this: there is no reason to go into battle with just one prong. My job for my patients isn't to give them a chance to win; it's to give them the absolute BEST CHANCE to win. I tell them I want to stack the deck in their favor. We often succeed because I get them to retry something they think failed, but at the SAME TIME adding in other prongs.

Self-health books, physical therapy, and support groups with other veterans or divorced parents can be another prong to help heal. Practicing daily gratitude, volunteering, joining a running club, and listening to a financial planner are prongs that can be part of the victory. What prongs you need to be involved in I will let you and your support system design. Remember, the problem was the army that DIDN'T show up, not the one that did. Imagine looking at that general and saying, nice job idiot, you failed. He would say, "Ah, don't blame me, I am the only one working here." To that same point, don't blame meds, counseling, or physical therapy, because they were tried but not at the SAME TIME in conjunction with other prongs. Why fight with one arm tied behind your back?

Maybe you can win with only one army, but why take the chance and put your resources together? There is data that medication with therapy is more effective together than one would anticipate by adding their combined effects separately. I'm a cancer patient. Surgery combined with chemo and radiation gives me the greatest cure rate for my type of cancer. I could have refused to use one or two of them, but why? I play to win and don't you also? It's also ok to win in a blowout. Why get only 20% better if you can get 80% by using multiple things? If you heal, why not heal faster?

Try physical therapy for your pain again but also try doing that non-narcotic-based pain medication that "didn't work" the last time. Pray again about your marriage, but add in marriage counseling. We need other things to get the first army back into the fight again. That's my story. I had been on and off medications for stress and anxiety in my life. It worked so so. I had never combined meds with a faith journey and individual professional counseling to help me heal fully. I added exercise in. Let's make your healing an all-hands-on-deck approach. With my cancer, it's all hands on deck. You would think I was a fool if my oncologist recommended surgery, chemo and radiation, but instead, I chose just one of those three.

Worse would be if I died, you decided that this proved that surgery doesn't work for cancer. No, it would prove I'm an idiot, don't worry though; I've proven that myself many times. Countless people can confirm that part. Maybe your "problem" seems small, and others are "making a big deal out of it," like that British general who thought Washington was a rebel not worth 3 armies. Well, let's just say there are a lot of "Washington streets, Washington high schools, and it's called Washington D.C." It is not called "a random British general no one remembers" D.C.

Because I brought countless prongs into my battles with anxiety and cancer, I can tell you I'm alive to write this book. This story isn't just my story; it's our story, science's story, God's story, and your family's story. It's how and why we fight. I want you to win and defeat those demons. We might be strangers, but what we have in common is greater than what divides us. We laugh, cry, love, win, lose, get angry and sit down for a bowel movement!

Chapter 11

We don't know S.H.I.T.

I pay special attention to things that were paid for in blood. The civil rights movement was paid for in the blood of countless African Americans. Our daily law and order gets bought in blood by the good officers of law enforcement. Whether you lean towards Black Lives Matter or Back the Blue, I promise you this: both sides' blood runs red when it's spilt. The same color my best friend bled on the day he died, trying to make this world a better place.

Speaking of making the world a better place, some feel it's going to shit right now. The origins of the swear word "shit" are quite fascinating, and it may be urban legend that it stems from a practical safety measure used by explorers during their journeys to far-off lands. When these explorers would land in foreign places, they needed to cultivate fresh food. To aid in this, they would carry crates of top-of-the-line fertilizer, which happened to be manure.

However, a problem arose when these ships spent weeks at sea with the crates of manure stored below deck. Sometimes, someone would venture below deck with a lantern to illuminate the area, unaware that the fumes from the manure had become aerosolized. When combined with the burning lantern, it caused unexpected explosions!

After several incidents, the cause of the explosions was discovered and a solution was devised. It was determined that transporting the manure on the ship's deck allowed the fumes to disperse harmlessly into the ocean air. As a result, the crates of manure began to be labeled with four words: "Ship High In Transit" or S.H.I.T.

Whether it is true or not, over time sailors recognized that these instructions indicated the presence of a valuable package in the crate. Thus, the term shit evolved from simple handling instructions to a popular little swear word with an intriguing history. Sometimes we only know part of the story. We may draw mistaken conclusions about someone based on the half of the story we know, or from our own perspective.

Let's talk about semis, air brakes and downshifting. In the song *Three Wooden Crosses*[17], Randy Travis says, "Semi-trailers don't stop on a dime." Trains, semis and other massive things are difficult to stop suddenly. In a car, we slam on breaks. A large semi-truck needing to stop suddenly uses multiple actions. One thing drivers are taught to stop safely is to downshift aggressively. Engines have multiple gears; when you go into a lower gear it limits the speed but slightly revs the engine until it slows. Higher gears at the same speed give a softer, quieter engine sound. So a vehicle at the same speed sounds louder in a lower gear. When a car is accelerating you hear the engine rev, but as it is automatically or manually shifted into a higher gear, you hear the engine briefly quieten as the car goes faster and then revs up again because the gas is still being applied. The reverse is true when you downshift, the engine will briefly get a bit louder but go slower.

At any given speed, going up a gear allows a vehicle to go faster and briefly quieter; going down a gear slows the vehicle but briefly revs the engine. In normal circumstances, with a semi, it is not something you usually notice as the driver slowly manually downshifts. If you have never driven a manual transmission, you wouldn't really know the inverse relationship between gear shifting and engine noise. Most vehicles only need their brakes to slow down emergently. If a semi-truck is trying to stop aggressively, they use downshifting to slow the truck down, along with other actions. It increases how quickly the semi can be slowed and augments that loud sound; if they're trying to stop very quickly it will cause the engine to rev very loudly. This creates an ironic situation because when you hear a semi-truck engine rev it could be downshifting to stop suddenly, as opposed to the usual engine rev we associate with speeding up. Because of its size and structure there is a great risk of stopping suddenly. It can jackknife or lose control. Controlling a semi safely is challenging. You can't use a singular data point (that of a loud noise) to know if the engine is speeding up or slowing down.

The tragic and unacceptable death of George Floyd in my home state of Minnesota was full of anger and hurt. I've talked about how anger is often justified, but we don't want to be controlled by it. There was justified anger in this situation. I was angry; everyone I talked to, including police officers, were angry. I've spent the past 20 years trying to understand better what my "white man privilege" looks like. I value diversity. My heart aches for people who don't look like me or have the same beliefs or sexual identity as I have, being treated poorly at times. I have a very special place in my heart for women, minorities, immigrants and many others who have not had white man privilege. I would be remiss not to call out that many social groups hurt in ways I never have; even if I haven't directly experienced firsthand I want to help heal it.

In the process of the protest that followed the death of George Floyd, the crowd overtook the I-35 interstate at one point. It led to a rapid attempt to get the interstate shut down for safety. I was nervous, hoping there would be no accidents. Watching live my heart sank when a semi-truck approached the crowd. I had no idea of the driver's intentions or what I was about to witness. My stomach felt nauseated, and I wanted to close my eyes as I anticipated horrific results. Miraculously the truck didn't kill anyone.

Some feel the driver was going into the crowd on purpose accelerating to hurt people, when I suspect the driver was trying to slow down and here's why. Part of the justification explained to me was that direct eyewitnesses, "heard the truck accelerate." I wasn't there, but again, based on noise alone you can't determine if a semi-engine revving is from pushing the gas pedal to accelerate, or aggressively downshifting to stop as quickly as possible. It would make the same sound. Knowing the engine was making a loud noise is only part of the story. You need to look deeper and watch what the truck itself was doing. Was the truck going faster, or was the truck going slower? You need two perspectives on this. The people there in person heard the sound of the engine, but I had a farther back approach that we saw on TV. With both data sets, you can better understand the meaning of the loud noise. I didn't know the driver's intention for certain, and this isn't meant to determine that. I know sometimes we need both sides of a story to realize if someone is trying to heal or hurt us.

There are many layers to the issues from that day which deserve much greater attention about how to heal as a society. It would be an injustice for me to try to pretend I know the answer. We need to heal systemic racism. We need police reform that holds those who abuse power accountable, and weeds them out before they commit further horrendous acts. We also need our police officers to feel respected. We need every person to feel safe at a traffic stop regardless of skin color. How to address these issues while still having respect for the many good people who serve in law enforcement or protest against injustice would take several books. I want to point out that listening and seeing different views helps one better understand what did or didn't happen on the bridge in those moments. Do any of us fully understand those few minutes? No, but if we work together, assume good intent and listen, we get closer to the truth. Direct witnesses say they heard the engine rev; from my bird's eye TV view, I think I saw the truck slow. Maybe if we listen to multiple perspectives, we can better understand the complex and important issues of racism, reform of our systems, and how to hold accountable both those who break the law (be it an officer or a citizen) but also love those who uphold it or were hurt by systemic racism. Certain police officers that week should be held accountable for what they did; others needed love and deserved respect. Furthermore some protestors needed to be held accountable for what they did; others needed love and deserved respect.

I thank the good law enforcement officers and protestors on both sides who wanted to feel safe and respected that week. I want to heal the hurt that bad police officers or unlawful protests cause. There are good and bad people on both sides of this situation. That week, most people on both sides simply wanted a better world and their families to be safe.

Chapter 12

We Rise or Fall Together,
So Let's Build a Bridge

B e it racism, police reform, pandemics, national debt, or elections; we are all in this together. Earth is the place we all call home. The most basic human endeavors of love, fear, hope, caring for family, laughing, and crying we all share. We need to listen to each other to heal each other. I hope the engine revving story can articulate how we sometimes don't know everything. We don't know the full story until we listen to someone else's perspective. Their life experiences and literal views from their position when something happened are often different from ours, but often essential to complete our picture.

To that end, let's continue with that fateful day.

The literal view I had from TV, plus past experiences driving vehicles that require manual shifting leads me to think that the revving was to stop the truck. I might be wrong. They heard the engine and they had a different literal view. Many of them have different past experiences than I do. However, no perspective of viewing something in the present or past is enough to understand things completely. When I speak about things I only state what I already know, but when I listen to someone I learn something I didn't know. I'm thankful that a situation I thought would result in absolute tragedy, with many people killed or injured, ended with much less harm.

I'm not stopping with the semi-truck driver. His story matters and so do the protesters' stories. I heard a hero amongst that crowd that I would love to meet someday; I want them to know that what they did may last generations.

The anger in that crowd was justified. George Floyd did not deserve to die that day. I've known many good police officers; I've seen a few bad ones. We become divided when we think we need to support or criticize the police (or protestors) without accepting we can do both. To heal, we must do both for both sides.

There was a second moment and a third when I thought I would see the tragedy from that day. I watched videos of that bridge from many angles to understand why the second one didn't happen. The terrified crowd pulled the driver out of the truck; it appeared he was going to be harmed. Some in the crowd were ready to seek revenge because of their anger. They were provoked over what happened to George Floyd and

Use the QR code to see the video.

afraid because they had feared for their lives seconds earlier. A genuine fear, regardless of the driver's motives, created an inflammatory situation. We have both fear and anger, two of the most combustible and dangerous emotions combined simultaneously. I expected to see a man beaten, but when I watched the video later I heard a beautiful voice. Someone said, "Don't hurt him; we don't want to be like that."

In a situation full of anger and fear, I heard love. When hurting was about to happen, I heard healing. I heard kindness and saw a crowd suddenly start to act differently. Love is the answer that wins over hate, anger and fear. It stops them from causing more hurt. People heard love, and they listened. You may or may not believe that thousands of years ago the Red Sea parted. I'm not here to convince you one way or the other on that. I can tell you though, I saw a sea part on a bridge near the Mississippi River that day. I saw a sea of anger and fear parted by love. Not all but some in the crowd were headed in one direction when suddenly they listened to love, to go a different way.

My heart sank not once, not twice, but three times. It took three of the most amazing miracles that I've ever seen. Somehow what I thought was about to become a bloodstained disaster became instead an opportunity to talk about healing. You need multiple perspectives to put it all together. A semi-truck was going to injure hundreds. A crowd was going to harm the driver. A police officer was going to be overrun by a crowd, and violence between the crowd and police would break out—three disasters all avoided in less than a few minutes.

I have a heart and an understanding for all sides in this situation. I'm not a minority. I'm not a police officer. I don't have a commercial driver's license. I haven't had a family member killed unjustly. I've never been in a situation without knowing if someone would be friendly to me at a traffic stop, or pull a weapon. This is something police officers AND people of color fear—whether they are being pulled over or doing the pulling over. I do know that to heal the hurting I need to hear from all sides. I know what unites us is greater than what divides us. We can all do better. I hope we listen to each other and gain wisdom; wisdom we can use to heal

Back to the point about the origin of swear words. It's funny how things sometimes have different meanings when you know the whole story. The worst situations can bring out the best in people. You may not realize it's their best if you don't see the entire story from all angles. Some point to problems with the police and some to the protestors in the aftermath of the horrible death, but they are focusing on smaller elements without realizing there were acts of kindness, empathy, and courage within both groups of people. Ever heard someone say, "You are full of shit?" Well, it turns out horse manure is an organic fertilizer. A bunch of horse shit can contribute to the vegetables we eat daily. If something as terrible as horse shit can transform something as amazing as vegetables, then the hurting of a tragic death can be turned into the healing of a city, a state, a country, and a world. A bloody death on a cross taught me how to love, even those I disagree with. I believe it's possible to support the concepts of Black Lives Matter and the ideas of Backing the Blue. The people in my state may be full of shit, but I think we can use that shit (or hurt) to grow some vegetables (heal) in all of us. We just have to love, listen, and learn.

Chapter 13

Parenting: Divorce and Death

There's too much to learn in life for us to go through it all by learning the hard way. In sharing my trials and tribulations more than my success, hopefully I save others some hurt. As you know, I have physical scars all over my body, two on either side of my neck and another on my chest. I have scars that go deeper, in places that no one sees unless I open up to them. I'm no different than you. You also have deeper scars, scars no one sees. Sharing emotional scars often involves reliving the hurt. I can point at the scar on my neck and not suddenly re-experience the physical pain of surgery. However, if I talk about failed relationships there is emotional pain I relive, things I wish I had done differently. Things I wish others would have done differently too.

I'm sorry if you're thinking about divorce, getting divorced, or already divorced. I know it's not how you envisioned things going and I don't know why you're here today. It might be because of someone else's actions. Out of nowhere you saw an e-mail or a text that made it clear you weren't the only person in your spouse's life. Maybe they laid hands on you or your children. Perhaps it was less sudden, a slow drift, and you "fell out of love." Maybe you were the one who messed up. I'm not here to tell you if divorce is the right thing or not. I don't know your situation. I walked a road I wasn't planning to. I am here to share a little about the path. Maybe my hurting and healing can help you hurt less and heal faster.

In my divorce, one thing I'm thankful for is that my ex-wife and I tried counseling. We didn't just "go through the motions," we truly gave it a sincere effort. We tried it more than once. Although the counseling didn't save our marriage, it did several other great things. It gave us peace to never have regrets. We tried as hard as we could. It made us both better at future relationships. My ex-wife and I get along better with each other because of it. I was just her "starter husband" anyways. Much like that first house that's a fixer-upper until you can afford something better; she's found a better fit. At

5 feet 7 inches with pale white skin, People Magazine isn't calling me for its sexiest man alive issue! In fact, during the pandemic I realized I looked better with half my face covered. Joking aside, I'm happy for my ex-wife; her new husband is probably an upgrade for her, and he had nothing to do with our relationship ending. As far as relationships with divorced spouses go, we have a reasonably healthy one.

Like a starter house with bad windows, we both fixed some bad habits and replaced them with newer, healthier ones we learned during counseling. New windows let more light in. Personal, family, or couples counseling can shed light on a dark area you are trying to find your way out of. It made us healthier going forward. Counseling wasn't wasted; I began to better understand relationship dynamics. This might come as a huge shocker, but It turns out that men and women think differently! Sadly, many people wait too long and go to counseling as a last resort. It's a check-the-box when you're already one foot out the door. They aren't fully engaged with it. The more engaged you are and the earlier you do it, the better chance it has. I encourage everyone to do it, but only if you are willing deep down to save the relationship and to grow. It is less effective if it's just to save face or prove to your spouse they are wrong and need to change. They may need to change, but we all can learn and grow. Why pay for counseling simply to tell your spouse they are wrong? That's what divorce lawyers are for.

Having done both, I know that counseling is a lot cheaper than a lawyer. Thankfully, we were both still invested in growing as people. Counseling extended our marriage by years, allowing us to get the amazing daughter we desperately wanted. It helps us co-parent better. That marriage led to an incredibly gifted daughter who is beautiful inside and out, and that counseling helped us help her reach her full potential.

Your relationship that either ended or is ending may not be because of divorce. It may be the death of a parent, child, sibling, or friend. I haven't lived that hurt, but I hope maybe a few lessons I learned along the way can heal. Thirty years ago as a child, something happened in our extended family that wasn't fair. It would make a person question where God is. I had an uncle who was one of the kindest and warmest men I ever knew. One morning, no different than any other, he went fishing for a short time, planning to spend the rest of the day with his wife and three boys. Sadly he would never return; he died unexpectedly from what I am guessing was probably a heart attack or pulmonary embolism. My kindhearted aunt suddenly had three boys to raise on her own.

Simply put, it wasn't fair to any of them. At that time, it made no sense. A great man was taken far too soon. Many in the family were hurt, confused, and even angry at what would happen. There was a void in that family they didn't deserve. I saw something in the "unfairness" of it. I saw three boys between the ages of 11 and 18 have to take on roles they weren't prepared for, deal with hurt they couldn't understand, and a mom taking on more than anyone could alone. What those challenges did though, just as iron sharpens iron, was to make that family closer and stronger. Those four wonderful people look out for and care more for each other than any family I know. They have different interests, abilities, and skill sets forged together in a fire of tragic loss that made no sense then. In hindsight, 30 years later, I see how that hurt turned into healing. I see a healed wound; the scar left in its place was stronger than the original skin it cut. I see these cousins of mine as brothers. I admire and speak highly of each one of them and my aunt. I see them fly across the country to help each other. I see them compromise to work as a team. I see days taken off work to spend six hours driving so that one of them can get a test done; I see them call each other and share their treasures of time, money, and skills with each other. I see it done at extraordinary levels. It's not "just what families do" for each other. No, it's another level. It's a level that is only reached when in adversity; people are pushed to places they didn't know they could go. It occurred to me once when someone asked, "Why would God do that?" Maybe we shouldn't blame God for what the devil did but thank God for picking up the pieces.

The loss of a parent or child too soon is a tragedy. It's hurting that destroys many people, but ironically it creates healing for some that lead to extraordinary outcomes. Countless charities and awareness campaigns were founded out of the death of a loved one. I have seen the souls of people live on by healing others because of the work their loved ones did. For example, Susan G Kolman and Jimmy Valvano are names you may know because in great personal loss, their loved ones were victorious over adversity.

Another interesting and surprising fact is when you look up the percentage of U.S. Presidents who lost a parent as a child or lost a young child, it's mind-blowing. Losing a parent is clearly NOT a good thing for a child. It should, and often does, leave people worse off. Losing a young child is clearly NOT a good thing for a parent; it should and often does negatively change their life. This fact is so startling in the number of presidents it has impacted, one would expect the number to be lower than the general population if it's a negative thing, which it clearly is. So why has it happened to so many of them? It's so disproportionate that this negative thing happened; there must be something that turns hurting into tremendous healing. If you think it's a small sample size oddity, think again. Look into other areas of incredibly high achievers, and you will see it. Someone is picking up the pieces of these shattered lives.

Unlike divorce, I haven't lived this. I hope never to live it, so I can't say in specific terms what exactly happens in this situation other than, generally speaking, this adversity helps them reach their full potential and climb higher. Gold is made most pure by heating it to an extremely high temperature that would destroy and burn up most things. So, do certain people become the best version of themselves, not despite, but maybe because of great loss?

I had learned this surprising fact about losing a parent or child twice in my life, each time many years apart. At first, I didn't think it applied to me and hoped it never would. Later I used it as a comfort that if I didn't come out of one of my cancer or heart surgeries, the conversations, teaching, and love I already had given to my daughter would still help her accomplish great things. I still use that as motivation today because I guess that BEFORE those parents died, what time they did have with their young children they made the most of. I realized that in a brief time teaching, loving, and leading those close to you with intent could have a greater impact than decades of just doing something halfhearted. Just recently though, I realized I was someone who is only reaching my full potential, not despite a death but because of a death. I should parent each day like it was my last; sometimes I need to put down the phone and be present with others. That email can wait; being a parent is way more important than any job I ever had, and trust me, the pay is better.

I mentioned at the beginning that my best friend died because his heart was too big. Just as high temperatures purify gold, his death was the fire that made me want to get rid of my imperfections. I will never completely get rid of my flaws. In his dying, though, he made me reflect on my flaws and want to live a life that honors him. If he was still with me today I might take him for granted, but in dying he leaves me the honor and responsibility of ensuring his memory lives on in the better parts of me.

Chapter 14

Parenting with Oreo Cookies and Snow Blowers

O reo cookies have two sides and a middle. When you need to have a difficult conversation with someone or share constructive feedback, it's often best to start with a positive reinforcement of that person—reaffirming the relationship by focusing on things you like about them, and they do well. This is good for personal and professional relationships. Trust me, you may have been "Oreo cookied" in your life and not even know it. It's not a trick, it's creating a safe situation to tell people something they don't want to hear, but you are doing it out of love.

Many avoid these difficult conversations altogether, missing a growth opportunity for someone they value. Sometimes though, we owe it to people close to us to have them. Thus, start with a positive. Then have a difficult feedback element and end again with a positive, so the takeaway is still about the value of the relationship. Positive first is the top of the Oreo cookie, the difficult part is the middle of the Oreo cookie, and then end with positive again, which is the bottom part of the Oreo cookie. Now if you are confused because the best part (the cream in the middle) is the difficult part, well I don't blame you, but I didn't come up with it, so let's just roll with it.

Here is my funny Oreo story. We were in a Minnesota snowstorm. The snow is several inches deep already, with more coming down. I did not want to leave the snow removal to my then-wife. I was in residency; we had a limited budget. I had a shovel and a small snow blower. As the snow blower was small, it did not have the best engine and was notorious for not starting in cold weather. It had a cord you could plug in for electrical starting when the rope you pulled wasn't enough. I had pulled and pulled and pulled on the rope many times this cold night. It was clear this snow blower would not start without being plugged in. The problem is it's 11:30 at night, and in this starter house we live in, there's no electricity in the garage.

DAVID WALKING WITH GRACE

If I wait till the next day when it's warm enough for the blower to start, there will be a foot of snow or more. Our house was on a busy street, so school kids would have to walk through the snow. I shoveled a lot, but knew I couldn't finish that night without the snow blower. Small snow blowers don't manage large snowstorms well unless you blow the snow part way through, clear it and repeat later. I have to work at 7 a.m. I need a snow blower to help with the work. That's when I come up with a great idea, I mean a terrible idea, no it's a great idea, no it's a terrible idea! I get this idea that only a man would think is great, but he instantly knows smart people (women) will hate it. Although the garage does not have electricity, the house does. I take this snow blower into the house and plug it in, so I can start it. Starting a snow blower in a house will make the house smell like gas for a while amongst other issues, for which any reasonable human being would probably have said I should not have done. But if you're reading this, you can guess which path I decided (and understand why said wife is now ex-wife).

My wife was upstairs as I brought the snow blower into the first floor. Quietly I got close to our front door. Like a criminal getting ready to leave a crime scene, I get bundled up in snow gear. My scheme for this crime was a snow blower plugged into an outlet in the living room; the getaway plan was via the front door. I review my "genius plan" to open the door and charge out the second the engine starts and before my wife realizes a small engine is running in the house. I'm smart enough to know she won't like it but dumb enough to go ahead with this crime against tranquility.

My poor ex-wife has no idea she's about to hear the roar of an engine inside her living room. I know she's not going to like it. I even briefly pause to reconsider if this is a good idea; six hours away from needing to be up in the morning for work, tired and exhausted, staring down several inches of heavy snow. I need to clear this portion of snow so that people can walk through it in the morning. So alas, I take the top part of the Oreo cookie, call upstairs and tell my wife I love her and know she won't like this next part, but I promise I'll make it up to her. Confused, she says what do you mean? The answer was the roar of the internal combustion engine from downstairs. My crime revealed she yelled at the top of her lungs, "That is not OK." She probably yelled a few other things, but I was running out the door, so I didn't hear the rest.

As the smell of gasoline filled the house, I completed my task of clearing the sidewalk.

In my mind, this was a Robin Hood crime. I am the hero clearing a path so children wouldn't have to walk through the snow. She isn't seeing me as a knight in shining armor oddly when I get back inside. I could argue; justify why I did what I did. However, she just got a gas-smelling house which is the middle of the Oreo cookie, and listening to that is also important. I can worsen a bad situation or complete the Oreo cookie's bottom half and apologize. I acknowledge I understand where she's coming from. I admit it wasn't my best decision. Having windows open in our house in the middle of January so that we can get the unpleasant smell out of our house confirms her side.

Challenges are bound to arise in various aspects of life, whether it's relationships, work, or society. It's important to acknowledge that there are often multiple perspectives involved. Sometimes, admitting that you were partially wrong is necessary while acknowledging your partial correctness. By actively listening to the other person's side, you allow them to recognize that you genuinely cared and paid attention despite being flawed. Admittedly, my wife wasn't entirely pleased with me. Our daughter was not conceived on that particular night. However, by genuinely considering her viewpoint, I alleviated some of her anger and helped her grasp my perspective to some extent. Did she fully agree with me? Probably not, but we managed to mend our relationship enough that I didn't have to spend the night on the couch.

Our first home taught us valuable lessons, including that even the best homes require periodic roof replacements. Like preventive maintenance on a water heater or furnace keeps our home warm and welcoming, other aspects of our lives also require proactive maintenance. This includes friendships or business relationships that may seem strong at the moment but still need ongoing care. Counseling can be one of the ways to maintain these relationships. It's important to understand that seeking counseling doesn't mean there's something inherently flawed in you or the other person. Like routine maintenance for a friendship or a water heater, it helps us avoid unexpected conflicts or breakdowns. It's highly likely that when you're close to someone for a long time, you or they will make a mistake, leading to anger or hurt. The goal is not to achieve perfection but to minimize the impact of these mistakes and maximize healing through apologies and forgiveness. Counseling doesn't have to be formal; it can involve talking to someone in your social circle who excels in healthy communication. Additionally, seeking information from positive sources such as podcasts, church messages, or Ted Talks can provide valuable insights.

You don't have to be hurting to consider counseling. You don't have to be thinking about divorce or telling off a friend for it to help. We all have a few issues in life that could be better. Counseling doesn't have to be only "to save a marriage" counseling, it can strengthen an already good marriage. Asking someone how you can be better doesn't mean you are bad. It is an opportunity to strengthen a foundation. The foundation of a home is the most important thing for its future—strengthen foundations with your friends, children, working colleagues, and spouses before the storm. Remember the Oreo cookie of starting with a positive, giving feedback, and ending with a positive. Remember to ask; as my wise neighbor told me, is this true, helpful, and kind to say. If not, reconsider. As my close friend reminds me, ask yourself if it needs to be said. Does it need to be said right now? Does it need to be said by me? These simple things you can practice enough for them to become the road your thoughts run down before you speak. Being quick to listen and slow to speak is a blessing; I am still learning today.

Feedback and how we give it is too important not to do. It can be the preventive maintenance that keeps us strong. It's that prophylactic healing that prevents hurting.

Chapter 15

Parent: What a True Apology Looks Like

People are either sorry about what they did or sorry for the repercussions. There's a difference between the two. Having experienced both situations I have learned to try to delineate the difference when others apologize. The reason isn't to determine whether I should or shouldn't forgive them. Either way, my healing involved forgiving them. I listen because I want to know if they are likely to repeat the behavior or if they learned from it. Past behavior predicts future behavior, unless we sincerely want to change. If they are only sorry about the repercussions and not for what they did, I may be hurt again. However if they are truly sorry, their healing can sometimes make them less likely to repeat. If you are in a physically unsafe situation, even if they are truly sorry and want to change, you first need to get to a safe place and have boundaries. If people are truly sorry they still may not be able to change. Change often takes a long time, and during this physical safety for everyone needs to be assured. If you create an unsafe situation, I want you to improve, but you must distance yourself and heal independently.

Regarding other types of hurt, I look for certain elements when I hear apologies. If you listen, you will be aware that some people are only sorry for the repercussions, not for what they did. They say sorry but slide in that they had the "right to have an affair." Excuses like their spouse was always working. They say they won't drink and drive again but say life stresses made them do it. They won't steal again, but they needed money for rent. I have transitioned from being sorry for the repercussions of my angry words toward others, to truly being sorry about my anger. I am sorry about the words, e-mails, body language, etc.

I am sorry, even when I didn't get in trouble for it. In many ways, I am more sorry about those times. It doesn't mean my behaviors have completely gone away. It means I am motivated to change them and have a plan. My future will look less like my past. We have to ask not only for others' apologies but also for ourselves. Here's how you know the difference in yourself; if you knew you wouldn't get caught or there would be no repercussions, would you do it again? Or even with zero punishment, would you still avoid the behavior in question. Do you speak about it in terms of "I did, I should have, I didn't," or is it, "She did this, he should have, they didn't"? We have to own it to heal ourselves; if others own it, we will continue to hurt others. If someone puts part of the blame on us, and they don't own it, they will continue to hurt us. Two people can both be wrong, but each must own their part.

It's important to know where you or the other person is at. A person who is truly sorry for what they did will be less likely to repeat it. The person who's truly sorry for what they did starts to reflect within themselves to see what they can do differently. Realizing the situations that make them want to drink, be angry, spend too much, cheat, steal, gamble, and look at images online will still be present, but they learn to use different behaviors to cope. Our world will shake us; we must decide when it does and how we respond. Do we respond like a can of pop or a bottle of water when shaken? A bottle of water quickly returns to its previous state without erupting (aka hurting someone). A can of pop lets the shaking cause it to remain stirred up for a long time; as soon as it is open it will erupt. It's not the shaking that causes the hurt; it's the response to the shaking. You can't stop yourself from being shaken; you can make yourself more like a bottle of water, though.

The hurt from gossip, someone letting us down, and harsh words don't magically go away when someone says they are sorry. Sorry doesn't truly heal anything unless the person saying it decides to heal themselves, and the person hearing it decides to allow healing to happen in them as well. If you take that hurt and learn from what you did (not what others did) wrong, you can flip the switch on the old saying, " You can't teach an old dog new tricks." I believe that saying is true if the person is only sorry because they got caught. If they reflect on what they did wrong and what temptations lead them astray, they can learn to respond differently when tempted. You can decide to block that website so you can't look at it, or start a budget so you can repay the money you owe someone.

Don't keep beer in the fridge, so when you are tempted to have one after a stressful day at work, there aren't any. The best person to design a security system for a bank is a reformed bank robber. It is up to us to decide to admit we robbed a bank; heal ourselves or just be mad we got caught and continue to hurt and blame others. Was it the cop's fault you got that speeding ticket, or could you have gotten up 15 minutes earlier? How you view that ticket will say a lot about how likely you are to get another one.

I pay attention to things that put the responsibility on the person who was hurt, versus the person who takes responsibility for saying it. "I am sorry you got offended by what I said" versus, "I am sorry that I said something offensive, I may not have meant it to be, but I understand now why it was." One person plans to keep talking similarly, hoping you wont hear it again. The other plans on not saying it again, regardless of who might hear it.

A true apology gives no disclaimer; the speeding ticket you were "only going seven miles over." These comments minimize our responsibility by trying to deflect accountability. Without personal accountability, you can't change. Also, true apologies include a change plan, which starts with you. If the plan is "if only you wouldn't" nothing changes, if the plan is "I will, or even if you do that I can respond this way instead" then change can happen. The most effective plans are usually multiple-pronged. Hurting someone can be simple, like forgetting someone's birthday, not returning a call, or much worse, but we all occasionally hurt others.

I also read and listen to others who have made similar mistakes to me in life, using their insight into how they changed. Harsh words aren't my only mistake in life, but I have to save something for future books, right?

Chapter 16

Physician: Have a Beer with the Doctor and BS

What's your favorite beer? Through trying different types of beer, wine or mixed drinks, many of us learned that we had certain versions we liked and served a certain way (cold versus warm). I remember not liking the taste the first time I had beer; I have heard that from others. For better or worse though, we weren't deterred. We soldiered on and didn't give up. We persisted down the liquid barley road, determined to use the proper combination of alcohol, flavor, and temperature to provide us with that magical elixir to produce such amazing dance skills or liquid courage. We persisted in our search for the grapes and learned that we like Pinot Noir or Riesling.

One of the challenges people face with cancer nutrition is finding a good supplement to help them get vitamins, micronutrients, protein, and calories. Many patients have told me that they understand the importance of getting these essential items, but they just can't stand the supplement's taste. I learnt from one patient that they had done a "taste test," and after a trial of a few different ones, they found one they could enjoy. Take this simple combination. Boost and Ensure are two major brands. Vanilla, chocolate, and strawberry are three I have tried. When you try each flavor, each brand, cold or warm, you have 12 options. My guess is if we give most of you 12 different types of beer or wine, there will be a few you wouldn't like but one or two that you could at least consider drinking on occasion.

Now there are more than just these two brands. There are also options from more liquid-based to more shake based. If you are about to start on this journey, are already on this journey, or have a loved one on this journey, I encourage you to continue finding a decent-tasting supplement. Like a college student who didn't like that cheap three-dollar keg beer that was warm, but years later enjoyed a beer or wine with colleagues after work; through trial and error you can find your drink or supplement of choice. So drink up, my friends! For yourself or a loved one, have a test tasting party. If you or they are in a hospital, often the supplements arrive barely chilled, but if you ask a nurse to put them in the fridge (or have a cooler in your room), you can enjoy them cold. This is often overlooked until it's too late; don't fall behind on nutrition.

Now that we have our drink let's BS. I mean Bristol Stool. If your name is Bristol, I apologize in advance for the fact that we are about to talk about the Bristol Stool Chart. In my defense I did not name it. That being said, doctors are weird people; we like to talk about poop so much that we need an entire chart about different types, known as the Bristol Stool Chart. If you don't believe me go ahead and google it. I encourage my fellow cancer or chronic GI symptoms patients to understand this chart. There are a couple of different animations of it. Believe it or not, the artistic abilities of the poop-drawing segment of medical artists vary somewhat. It's crazy that someone could say they are good at drawing poop on their resume. Science majors used to make fun of art majors in college, but they are bailing us science dorks out now so we can talk about poop!

Now that you've googled the Bristol Stool Chart and you're looking at different types of poop, be careful because if your boss walks by your desk, they will wonder what you're up to. You may think you're safe because you're at home, but then there is that browser history... I promise there's a method to my madness. Different types of stools on the chart help give insight into many things, like the degree of constipation, lack of fiber, etc., that you might be dealing with. Cancer patients frequently end up on narcotics or other medicines that impact their GI tract. Many people with chronic abdominal pain have motility issues in one direction; to be clear, it's the same direction, but either too much or too little. To minimize symptoms, being proactive and paying attention to how often you're having a bowel movement, how hard you're straining, and the type of stools you're producing helps you stay ahead of the game. With my cancer, I proactively monitored my bowel movements and types. It allowed me to titrate the available over-the-counter medicines proactively. Like supplements, the downstream effects of not having good control of bowel movements can be detrimental, with diarrhea causing dehydration and constipation causing nausea. This is serious shit, so stop laughing!

BRISTOL CHART

Figure 1
(Constipation)
Individual pieces, somewhat like nuts.

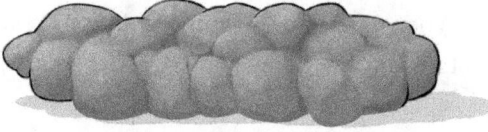

Figure 2
(Constipation)
Referred to as "sausage shaped," still lumpy.

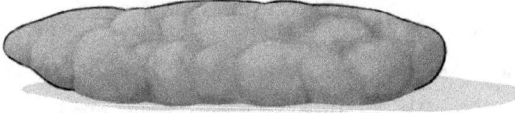

Figure 3
(Good / Ideal)
Sausage-like with lumps, but stays together when passing.

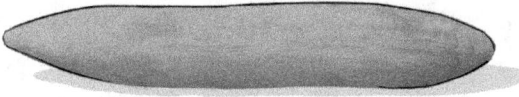

Figure 4
(Good / Ideal)
Smooth and soft, like toothpaste.

Figure 5
(Good / Loose)
Large soft pieces that are passed easily.

Figure 6
(Loose / Diarrhea)
Sometimes called "fluffy", pieces have distinct shapes, but overall it's mushy.

Figure 7
(Diarrhea)
A brown water-like liquid, known as diarrhea.

This information will empower you to be a stronger advocate for yourself or your family. If you notice stools suggesting constipation or diarrhea, note the frequency of bowel movements. It helps you use your already prescribed medicines or contact your healthcare provider. I've seen patients wait too long to address these issues, and end up in situations where they have abdominal pain or nausea, or wait too long to treat a possible infection causing diarrhea. You don't have to be a cancer patient to benefit from this. I have many people tell me their stools are normal. When I pull up the chart and they show me which one, I say, "Yeah, that's not normal." My boss knows I google poop pics, and it's ok; I can't promise what your boss will say!

It might make for a good party trick, also. Impress your friends when they're sitting around at that baby shower by saying I used to be a Bristol type 1, but after researching, I'm now at Bristol type 4. You want to say it in your most fancy and elegant voice ever. When they ask you what a Bristol type 1 versus 4 is, you can explain that only the most refined individuals can speak in such elegant terms. Encourage them to google a Bristol Chart. Then watch and laugh when they realize what you're talking about. Wrap it up with a bit of discussion about fiber or PRN[18] bowel meds, and you can help your friends out one poop at a time! On more than one occasion, people have traveled hours to have their chronic abdominal pain, nausea, and diarrhea evaluated by me, and in five minutes, with the stool chart and simple education about fiber, stool softeners, medication side effects, hydration, etc. we solved the suffering they have spent years dealing with.

I've tried to milk as much humor as possible from this practical advice related to nutrition and bowel issues.

The truth is there are several other issues I want to share with people that should be helpful to know and be aware of. Is this education already out there? As we say in Minnesota, "You betcha!" Here's the problem; it comes in a 49-page handout with complex terms people struggle with during one of the scariest moments in their lives. My goal here is to put bureaucracy aside and help you learn, laugh, and in love to heal the hurting of cancer.

If you're having trouble swallowing, be proactive. Many medicines are available in either a liquid or a softer version. Ask your care team about this.

Busy providers don't always automatically think about it, but we can change this as soon as it comes to mind. Another med point, ask specifically about which meds can cause sedation, from your current and new ones. Cancer patients sometimes end up on pain medications that will cause sedation but can still be taken safely. It can become dangerous because sometimes people don't know which medicines sedate them and take multiples at once. People often know pain and sleeping meds, but nausea, anti-itching, or anxiety meds may also have these effects. Patients often have multiple cooks in the kitchen, a surgeon, a medical oncologist, a primary care provider, and Waldo. No, Waldo isn't in this book, and no one knows where Waldo is; these sedating meds are already confusing enough. My point is that the doctors may not know that you are suddenly on 4-5 meds that could cause sedation, because each professional added another one. Knowing which ones cause it is half the battle. The next half is the first few times you take a sedating med; watch how you feel for a few hours before you try another one. Have a loved one close by to keep an eye on you. The last thing your mom with breast cancer needs is to fall in the bathroom and break her arm because she is too sedated. Sedation is one side effect; dizziness and dehydration that are "different," may in combination make the two side effects worse.

Cancer medications become complex. Mixing in sedation and it becomes easy to forget which ones you've taken or haven't. Making yourself a checklist box or table where you write down the medicines and the times can be very helpful, especially starring the sedating ones.

Having someone else monitor your meds can be helpful. Even if you don't have someone who lives with you or close by to a loved one, thankfully, with technology such as smartphones, you can just take a picture of your medication chart or FaceTime them, and they can set a phone alarm. These principles don't apply just to cancer patients; again I have had people travel long distances or experience "problems" that I could make go away with a dose decrease or stopping a medication. If you think a particular medication is an issue please talk to your doctor first, as simply stopping a medication without their input is sometimes as dangerous as starting one without their input!

Chapter 17

Parent, Physician, and Patient: HPV

In the song *Desert Road* by Casting Crowns[19], there is a powerful line that resonates with me: "I don't want this pain to be my story." Having undergone the challenges of illness myself, I understand that we cannot heal all pain and suffering.

I bear the scars on my neck from undergoing radiation twice, leaving me with difficulties swallowing and a chronically dry mouth. These long-term issues also pose the risk of jaw necrosis and bone death in the future.

However, for the pain I've endured from battling two cancers to have meaning, it must serve a greater purpose in healing others. The greatest healing possible is preventing others from experiencing the same pain. The best way to combat cancer is to ensure it never takes hold in the first place.

I don't want my pain to define me, but rather to motivate me to contribute to a world where suffering is minimized. Through our efforts to prevent and increase awareness, we can aspire to create a future devoid of the crippling impact caused by cancer.

Others suffer the same fate even though they don't have to. My cancer is now preventable. The HPV virus caused it. There is a vaccine for several of the HPV strains that cause cancer. When the vaccine first became available, I was not eligible originally. As is often the case, over time, we learn more, such as expanding treatment to other situations. Thankfully I am now eligible for the vaccine. HPV landed two very hard punches. Punches that took me away from time with my daughter, and being able to work on healing others. Instead of being able to care for myself and my daughter, there were times when I needed others to help care for us.

HPV, you knocked me down, but you picked a fight with the wrong guy! You tried to kill me twice. You should have finished me when you had the chance. Too bad for you; some good Samaritans came along and saved my life. In my first round, I was just another patient at the health system that treated me. I didn't work there in 2017. A few years later, I was humbled to be hired by that same health system and call these wonderful doctors, nurses, social workers, managers, support staff, and others my colleagues. After a second dance with the beast, the little virus capable of causing cancer, I am getting up off the mat. I am on the "indentured servant" plan, since I now work at the place that saved my life. Each week my paycheck from them reads the amount of, "We saved your life, dude, nuff said." Thankfully for me, it's not exactly like that, but these strangers (good Samaritans) that saved my life are now colleagues of mine.

I consider these former strangers not just colleagues but friends. So HPV, we are going to kick your gluteus maximus. My friends are coming along with me. They just don't realize it yet.

The first friend I'm bringing along is my daughter, my favorite person to spend time with. I thank God science has provided humanity with a gift for her that was not available to me at her age. She will get the vaccine to prevent her from the horrible atrocities of this virus. We can prevent her from needing to have her neck cut into, radiated, and poisonous chemotherapy administered. It's a parent's obligation to protect their children.

When people look at their children and think about the HPV vaccine, they must realize that this virus is coming after them. Estimates vary, but 55 to 90% of people, as adults, will get the HPV virus if not vaccinated. Initially, there was an assumption that this was transmitted through sexual activity *only*. Understandably so, when this issue of the vaccine came up, people were talking about vaccinating their children from a sexually transmitted disease. This created some uncomfortable situations for parents. Quite frankly, the rollout of the initial vaccine was terrible. As a member of the larger scientific field, we got it wrong. Science introduced a term I had never heard of until this vaccine, a "sexual debut." It was thought one needed to have this vaccine before becoming sexually active. This was wrong based on what we now know, but unfortunately the term sexual debut was out there. It makes it sound like it's a Broadway musical, with the lead role getting together to celebrate with friends and family afterwards. The first time I read and heard of that term in medical literature, I winced. NO! Parents, this has NOTHING to do with when or what age your child will have their first sexual encounter and EVERYTHING to do with not letting them be harmed. This is about cancer, plain and simple. Cancer. Cancer, and Cancer! Alas, let me try to undo two decades of misunderstanding.

First, getting or not getting this vaccine isn't going to be on their minds when someone decides to be sexually active. The last time you were sexually active, did you choose based on you or your partner's HPV vaccine status? Was your partner pouring you a glass of wine as you listened to romantic music? As they rubbed your back, you still weren't in the mood to be intimate, but when they whispered into your ear, "I'm vaccinated," suddenly, like Meg Ryan in *Top Gun*[20], you yelled, "Take me to bed or lose me forever?" The wine, song, and back rub might have played a factor, but no one whispered their vaccine status! Or, on the flip side, if you are extremely angry at your partner and they are about to sleep on the couch with no chance of intimacy but say, "BTW, I got the vaccine today," do you suddenly go from uninterested to captivated? Many things prevented me from having sex in high school, including the lack of a girlfriend! I was a short, shy kid, and all the vaccines in the world wouldn't make me tall, dark, and handsome. This is not about sex; it's about cancer. This is why I am not in any way, shape, or form talking about waiting till marriage, abstinence, safer sex or any of the other various issues around sexuality.

Second, even if you are a nun or monk and have lived a life of no sexual activity, you can still get the virus. Data suggests, for example, that cauterizing done during medical procedures can be a transmission route. Other data indicates more casual non-sexual contact can pass it on. Again a majority of adults get this. This is not about sex; it's about cancer. My radiation oncologist, who I enjoy seeing but just wish it was under different circumstances, is one example of someone with a theoretical work risk. An OB-GYN or head and neck cancer surgeon might also.

This is not about our 10-15-year-old daughter or son today. This is about their future 10, 20, and 30 years from now. This is about how parents do countless things over decades to prepare their sons and daughters to be in the strongest position possible as an adult. I will not speak about other vaccines. If your child gets HPV-related cancer as an adult, I don't want you to have regret because, as healthcare providers, we didn't do as good of a job explaining things. The cancer comes decades after exposure. My parents wish they could have gotten me the vaccine, but it wasn't an option back then.

I do this to prepare my daughter for adult life in the same way I show her how to do laundry, save, give to others, fix a flat tire, how to read and prepare her to fight the unforeseen adversities life will throw at her. This is about countless acts to protect them from harm. This is about telling HPV, not her, not him, not now, not today, not ever! You don't get to hurt this one. This is about not letting someone take a knife to your child's neck in 15 years, even if it is a surgeon cutting out cancer. This is about your child not choking to death on their dinner because their swallow is impaired by radiation. This is about them not bleeding to death alone in an apartment after cancer surgery. You have two choices, let this virus take a free shot at inflicting immense emotional, physical, financial, and relationship pain on your child, or stand up to cancer. Not everyone who gets the virus gets cancer, but why let it have a free shot?

To my healthcare friends, parents aren't the main issue here. We are, in large part because it's a unique situation. Case in point: would you give me the HPV vaccine? I have had HPV cancer, so I am already exposed, you may think? A reasonable thought, but actually, the answer is, YES you should. Why, because I had ONE of the high-risk types years ago, but the vaccine covers multiple high-risk types...

Protect me from those. Next question: would you vaccinate someone in a monogamous relationship, married for 20 years? YES! Again it can be transmitted in nonsexual ways. Plus, sometimes a spouse dies far too soon, a divorce happens, or the person who thinks they are in a monogamous relationship isn't. When you factor in all these variables, it's a no-brainer. This is about CANCER. We must stop thinking about what someone is or isn't doing in their bedroom. We have been getting this wrong for years. Recommendations keep expanding, although at no previous time in my life was I eligible for the vaccine, I am now. Recent guidelines now extend to anyone in their 40s. This pain is my story; I don't want it to be yours or your children's.

Chapter 18

"In the middle of difficulty lies opportunity."
- Albert Einstein

T his quote is engraved on a rock two friends gave me in college. Miraculously 24 years later, I haven't lost that rock. For a man to keep track of anything for over 20 years that isn't permanently attached to his body is a rare feat... There is also a picture of a man next to a cake that has also made this journey. That man's family we talked about earlier, in chapter 13. Before I tell the story of this rock, I must tell you about my freshman year of college.

In January of that year, a friend had this "great idea" for a challenge. For one month straight, we should try to socialize every night. It was foolish; something only a teenage mind would think was good. I didn't think it was good. No, I thought it was great! Teenagers don't have fully developed frontal lobes; some would say men at any age don't. We were proving these points in our "challenge." So dumb and dumber start on their journey. I want to protect the innocent, so I will not say which friend this was. It wouldn't be fair of me to talk about what a dumb 18-year-old suggested to me years later. Embarrassing myself is fine. Making fun of my dumb decisions is ok, but I can't do that to my friend Ed; he is too nice!

Our college had J-term, a one-month course. You take one class every day, several hours in class. Having class start around noon gave us foolish 18-year-olds the idea that staying out till the late hours in January, would earn us a badge of honor.

Twenty-plus years later, as I retell this with more wisdom, I am not proud of it, but we had "successfully" reached double-digit nights of going out. For whoever sat next to us in that class freshman year, I apologize, as not once at this point had we showered before class. We woke up, threw hats on and headed off. If we had "extra time," we brushed our teeth; if not, well priorities!

Somehow, both of us were single at this point. Surprising, as we were real catches, a couple of science majors showing up each day unshowered. Shortly after our streak reached double digits, my dad intervened. Technically his kidney intervened. I would get a phone call in January that took my breath away. My dad, 45 years young, had cancer. How we came to this diagnosis is compelling, funny, and scary.

For this part, we have to go back to the farm I grew up on and the perils of living in Minnesota during the winter. Our driveway is a half-mile from the road to the house, with nothing but fields on either side. It's essentially an old country dirt road. Subject to driving winds and snowdrifts, there is no shelter on either side. Snowdrifts made our driveway impassable at times. Even when drivable, ice patches made it slippery. The barren winter fields, though, do need their fertilizer. Earlier, we explored the amusing origins of fertilizer, and in the winter of my freshman year my dad was out with his farm equipment spreading fertilizer (manure). As part of the process, he ended up near the edge of our property, having turned off the frozen half-mile driveway with the tractor still fully equipped with the spreader.

He suffered a life-threatening farming accident involving the power take-off shaft on the tractor. A device that can generate tremendous force to power equipment, but is also one of the most dangerous in farming; it has taken several farmers' limbs and lives. A power take-off (PTO) shaft running at 1,000 rpm; if it gets a hold of a person, can spin them around 16 times a second. When he got caught, this device, besides tossing him all around, also ripped his clothes off, leaving him in nothing but a pair of boots! Worse yet, it wound the final shreds of clothing so tightly around his forearms, it bound them together in a death grip. Now badly injured, my dad is a naked man half a mile from shelter on a cold day in Minnesota. His life was in peril from his injury and the weather. Worse, his arms were tied together, and he couldn't drive the tractor. He was hurt; in dire circumstances, and he could have died.

First, he tried to flag down a car he could see from the road for help. Now I want to preface this next part by letting you know my dad is still alive today, and the story ends well. Although it wasn't funny at the time as a man's life was in danger, imagine yourself in that car. You're driving down the road, commenting to your spouse how lovely the snow-covered fields look, when suddenly you see a naked man with his arms tied, trying to get you to pick him up. Oddly this car did not stop! To this day, we have a debate in the family; some say they just didn't see him, others say they were heartless. I somewhat comically question if you saw a naked man who looked handcuffed because of how his arms were bound, your first instinct probably wasn't to let him hop in your car and say, "Tell me about your day, friend." If they saw my dad, they probably thought he was mentally deranged and a danger to them, not realizing his life-threatening situation. Humor aside, this was as real as possible; my dad was in great peril.

My injured dad begins a treacherous, cold walk up the half-mile of driveway to our house for shelter. He's stumbling; arms tied like a prisoner, and in pain. He could have died. At one harrowing point, he slipped and fell on the ice. With his arms bound, it wasn't easy to get up. He told me how he

thought he might die and wasn't sure he would get up. He is fighting pain, fatigue, and frigid temperatures, hoping not to freeze to death. My mom and brother are sleeping only hundreds of feet away, and I am hours away in the dorm, all totally unaware of his dire situation. My dad's life was in danger; at a time when cell phones were rare, he had no way of getting help. It is still surprising to me he didn't die that day. My dad and I have since talked about how God can turn hurt into healing. As he completes his near-death march, he finally stumbles into the house. It occurred to me how dangerous this was, how scary it must have been, and how we each had a near-death experience alone without anyone around us. It makes my heart sink, but thankfully he lived. Like any loving son, I will share the other embarrassing part of this story.

It was a weekend morning, and my brother had a friend stay over. Unfortunately for my brother's friend, he was awake and watching TV. His Saturday morning was interrupted by a side, or multiple sides of my dad that he never planned on seeing. Like all of us, he is oblivious to what happened; my dad walked into the living room wearing nothing but a pair of boots! Arms tied, he looks at this poor kid who jumped up and said something we won't repeat here. It's no wonder he thought my dad was crazy. Talk about a traumatic sleepover for a kid.

Ok, we have made enough fun of my dad. My brother's friend quickly realized that my dad had been badly injured. He then woke up my mom and she rushed my dad to the hospital. Thankfully, none of his injuries were life-threatening. After imaging and tests, he was discharged and told everything was OK, which it kind of was. The next day he was bruised black and blue from shoulders to knees and purple from all the damage to his body. Not surprisingly, there was blood in his urine that day.

Now you may wonder why I would share the portion of the story, where my dad is injured at the end of our driveway and walks into the house naked. It's not just to get him back for all the embarrassing things he did to me when I was a kid! (Parents who embarrass their kids may find themselves in a book their kid writes one day). It's the blood in his urine. As a doctor, I discover blood in people's urine analysis frequently. Often it is microscopic; the patient isn't even aware. You only find it on the urine analysis. Usually it ends up being nothing serious, but it can be a sign of cancer. It can also be from recent trauma or surgery, a menstrual cycle, or a kidney stone, amongst other things. Doctors don't usually get too excited; we just ask that patients follow up to ensure it clears up and goes away.

Thanks to the diligent efforts of an internal medicine doctor who followed up on the case for several weeks, my dad was eventually diagnosed with kidney cancer. This serves as a crucial lesson for both patients and healthcare providers. When blood is present in the urine, it is essential to pursue a further investigation to ensure it is addressed and have a follow-up plan to ensure it is resolved.

My dad had two reasons for blood in his urine: the trauma he healed from and the more serious cancer. What could have killed my dad saved his life. In his hurting, there was healing for him and others. Microscopic blood on a urine analysis is often overlooked. A busy provider has 12 items already to address, and they can easily forget to remind you to get that follow-up, or to look back and realize it isn't going away. I can help you advocate for yourself and your family by discussing this. In today's world, most of us can view our test results.

During this time, I would come home from college. Two things stand out. I was doing chores in the barn all by myself. The younger me was of the mindset that men needed to show strength and not cry. By myself, doing the work and realizing my dad may need extra help in the coming days, and with the possibility of death looming, got to me. I began to cry. My dad walked in and saw his 18-year-old son struggling with the gravity of what the family was facing. Tears in my eyes, I tried to wipe them away suddenly, but he embraced me with a huge hug. In his arms, the tears turned to deep sobbing.

I'll never forget what he said while holding me in his arms. His voice cracking, he said that the hardest part of the cancer journey was seeing its impact on his loved ones. He was less afraid of his own circumstances but more worried about how it may impact his family. Years later, that would resonate with me when I became a father. I realized I was not so afraid of dying as I was of my daughter growing up without an earthly father. In my hurting that day in the barn, there was healing. I would learn it was ok to cry; it was therapeutic. I learned that keeping it in prevents healing and bonding.

The day of dad's surgery also stood out. First, I remember my grandpa saying to the surgeon, "May God bless your hands." At this point, faith is a small part of my life. I'm surprised I remember those specific words. The other thing I remember is one of my aunts coming to tell me how proud she was of me. She couldn't believe that as a still teenage "adult," I could comfort others and keep everyone calm during this difficult time. I probably appeared calm to the outer world because I was healing others. Don't forget, letting your family and friends help you may be a part of their healing and peace. I am more comfortable caring for others than needing others to care for me. My focus on healing led to me compartmentalizing my own emotions.

Later that day, I heard a song called *My Father's Eyes* by Eric Clapton[21] on the radio. The line "I am like a bridge that was washed away, my foundations were made of clay" lead to another flood of emotions.

At that moment, I realized I could lose my father, who, along with my mother, was a major foundation in my life. I think 25 years later, it's important to ask ourselves what are the foundations of our life in terms of our happiness or wisdom. Does happiness come from people who may die, or do we lose when a friendship or marriage ends? Is happiness in a sports team that may disappoint us? Is it by living vicariously through a celebrity or our children? What are the foundations for wisdom, or how to face a difficult circumstance? Do we have to turn to an earthly source of happiness and wisdom that may not always exist? I've realized Jesus can bring me joy even when I am single and facing cancer. If I die, my daughter will always have scripture for wisdom. Even if you aren't a believer in Jesus, the lessons Jesus taught have real practical everyday applications. So do parts of the Old Testament. Like many, I struggle with the Old Testament, but Proverbs is incredible. It has taught me many things, for example, "*A gentle answer deflects anger, but harsh words make tempers flare.*" (Proverbs 15: 4).

I do enjoy sports and value my earthly relationships with friends, family, or significant other. They aren't the foundation on which my life is built today, but they were in the past. I had experienced the hurt when relationships ended, or I had too much of my life centered on things like sports, elections, or living vicariously through others. I realize those things should be a part of my life but not the foundation. Build your foundation on something that will survive the storm. The foundation of a house isn't the part you enjoy; it's the part meant to hold up the portion you want to enjoy. We enjoy our living rooms, kitchens, bedrooms, and other parts of our house for various things, from sleep to delicious food. However, the foundation is the thing that holds everything else up in the house, and so for me having the right foundation in place maintains that balance. However, if the living room or kitchen of life becomes too big, it pushes out other things. If a sporting event causes us to miss visiting a family member, or a weekend shopping spree prevents us from putting anything into our savings account that month, suddenly, they start to turn the foundation of life into clay.

Just like Eric Clapton's song ended, so did dad's surgery. In the process of coming home, my freshman year "socialization" during January also ended for me. That January, I started to think about maybe going in a different direction with my life. As a freshman, I planned to be an athletic trainer or physical therapist to be around sports culture. I didn't think I was smart enough to be a doctor. Suddenly the idea of being a doctor became interesting to me. Dad's story would only be half the reason I became a doctor, but others would be healed as well.

Once I did become a physician, this little caveat of the blood in my dad's urine turning his hurting into healing would be a crucial lesson. I teach future physicians the story of his cancer. Urine analysis is a funny thing in medicine; frequently misinterpreted or misunderstood. Besides blood, there are also things like an enzyme called leukocyte esterase that may or may not themselves mean something—frequently looking at other data points plus the patient's symptoms and history in order to fully interpret these multiple findings. People's actions when we interact with them also sometimes require us to know their history, and what "symptoms" they are dealing with that day. The coworker who snapped may have just miscarried last night. The person who doesn't view police or doctors the same way you do may have had a history of being saved or mistreated by one or both of these professions.

As mentioned, blood in a urinalysis (UA) is somewhat common. I share this so you can be part of your own healing via the early detection of problems.

Providers forget to advise patients because they are overwhelmed, or patients get busy and forget what they were told. Life can be that way. A spouse may honestly forget you told them something or a busy family member may simply have had so many calls to make they were distracted and forgot your birthday. You might forget you were told this. If anyone reading this, looks up their records and sees blood in their urine; remember it is PROBABLY nothing serious, but reach out to ask your team if you need to get a repeat check-up to ensure it goes away. We often give it a few weeks. Let the stone pass; the trauma heal; the menstrual cycle end; and repeat it in a few weeks. It usually clears; however, I have seen people present where that follow-up never happened. They had blood in their urine many months or even a few years before meeting me. Not always, but on more than one occasion when I investigated it, we had a problem that earlier detection would have been beneficial. I tell my dad's story to many providers because a personal story makes us remember better. I also draw an analogy better for an occasional unpleasant comment or bad day, versus a person you repeatedly have to make excuses for. If blood persists on a UA it needs to be addressed; if you are always justifying someone's actions or needing to defend them, it may be a sign of a deeper, more serious problem.

To conclude, this personal story highlights how my dad's life was saved by something that could have ended it. Despite the pain, I hope that his experience can help healing. I also hope that you can learn to advocate for yourself better in life and the healthcare system through laughter. Of note, this blood in urine is one of various issues that may not be urgent at present but still require follow-ups; pulmonary nodules, borderline blood pressure, slightly abnormal labs and colon polyps, to name a few, are also issues that proactively using electronic access to help advocate can lead to preventive healing.

I suggest you make an appointment if you have something that sending messages in a chart or e-mail isn't a good way to discuss these things. By sharing these experiences, I intend to empower you to become a more effective advocate, which may require making a few more appointments to allow time for each issue. Healthcare providers are often overwhelmed, overbooked, and squeezing 12 things into 20-minute appointments isn't how we best achieve success.

It is a collaborative effort that your health deserves. Amidst the challenging journey up that driveway, there was an opportunity to detect my dad's cancer and for me to contemplate a new purpose in life. Thus, "In the middle of difficulty lies opportunity," a saying two close friends found important enough to engrave on a stone for me.

Chapter 19

Patient: Not One, but Two Parents

U nfortunately, my sideline learning about medicine would continue just a few months later. Still a freshman, five months after my dad's cancer diagnosis, I got a call again; this time my mother was diagnosed with cancer. Don't worry; my mom has no stories of her running half-naked! I would need some intense therapy if that were the case. An important part of my journey to become a physician occurred during my mom's cancer. As I went into the summer between my freshman and sophomore year of college, I decided to take a year off to spend time with my family and work to help pay the medical bills.

This led to one of the biggest arguments that I've had with my parents. I was determined that I was staying home; they were determined I was returning for my sophomore year. All three of us are stubborn and not known to back down in arguments. Alas though, I had the upper hand. I told them I was 19, a legal adult, and there was no way they could force me to return to college. Proud of myself, I thought the conversation over. That's when my mom played her ace card. She told me that was fine; they owned the farmhouse and I would not be welcomed in it. Staying home from college meant renting someplace else and being unable to help with chores. Mom and I are both good at math. She knew as a 19-year-old that if I got a job and paid for an apartment, food, etc., there would be very little left over for me to help my parents. Well played, Mom!

She too, was thinking about the foundation of my future, knowing regardless of how many years they would have on this earth, she wanted me to learn things I didn't already know, to invest in things that could impact our family even after we finished the battle at hand. I didn't have the experience of her wisdom to understand, and I disagreed with her. However, I could do the math, and in terms of immediate cash flow I was better off returning to campus, where grants and student loans covered the tuition, room, and board.

Humbled by Mom's ace card, I was also frustrated. I was convinced I would have only taken one year off and returned to college. My parents had the experience of knowing that things could go in a different direction during that year off. I might never return. They had the wisdom to know about stumbling blocks, and not everyone returns to college. At this point, cancer had picked its second fight with our family. Mom isn't just a smart cookie who loves her sons. She is also tough as they make them. She won that round, and the score is now the Boeders 2, Cancer 0.

Now we are really living out, "In the middle of difficulty lies opportunity." Those horrible occurrences in life that can make a person at that moment question God's existence, or make them angry with God, may just be the greatest blessing in our life. There is a difference between this and a quote that's often used and is similar to it. The quote is, "What doesn't kill you, makes you stronger." I like Einstein's quote better. It's more accurate to say that difficulty creates opportunity. People grow in difficult times, but not always stronger. It is our choice which way we grow. It is an opportunity to grow angrier, grow quicker to judge, and to stop listening to others. It is also an opportunity to grow more thankful and to see everyone suffering in some way or facing some battle, so you grow more empathic. It is an opportunity to grow in love and to reflect on past mistakes. The choices we make are the opportunity to become stronger or weaker. The opportunity to yell more and hurt or listen more and heal.

Our past experiences are valuable lessons, but it's important to recognize that they can also influence our perceptions and judgments in future situations, especially if we have been hurt. Learning from our failures is crucial, but we shouldn't let them instill excessive fear that prevents us from trying again.

What doesn't kill us has the power to shape us. It allows us to love more deeply or to harbor more hatred. It gives us a chance to rely on our own strength or to trust others. It offers the choice to laugh at ourselves humbly or mock others with cruelty.

By understanding the impact of our past and embracing the lessons learned, we can navigate future encounters with a balanced perspective. It's about finding the right balance between caution and resilience, learning from the past while allowing ourselves to move forward with courage and an open heart. I now pay attention to similar behavior in other people or myself. Many of us, myself included, often repeat mistakes at work and in our personal lives. I learn when there is a similar pattern to a situation I am in or the person I was before. I also give each person and situation a fresh opportunity.

Chapter 20

Scars

Scars possess a fascinating duality, representing both the process of healing and the memory of pain. Remarkably, the tissue that forms a scar often ends up stronger than its predecessor. However, this strength can pose challenges when surgeons revisit a surgical site years later, as the dense scar tissue can be difficult to navigate. In such cases, the hardening of scars can have negative implications.

Nevertheless, there are instances where scars take on a beautiful quality. Similar to how an oyster produces pearls in response to internal damage, scars can be a narrative of one's journey. They become a means to share personal stories and contribute to the healing of others. It's important to acknowledge that scars are always born out of physical or emotional pain and can inspire and connect individuals on a deeper level.

My mom and dad would both have additional cancer issues; counting my two, the score is Boeder family seven and cancer zero so far! I'm not saying this to brag. Cancer still has the opportunity to continue to come after us; one score is a lethal win. It left scars from the various treatments that we have received. I am thankful for the scars. In the song *Scars* by I Am They[22], "I am thankful for the scars, cause without them I wouldn't know your heart." When I listen to it with surgical scars on both sides of my neck, plus a scar on my chest, I realize surgeons have cut into me four times, each surgery was meant to save my life: each side of my neck to access cancer, and twice into my chest because of my heart. I really need to look into BOGOs on surgeries, or at least four for the price of three.

In addition to having had cancer twice, I have a genetic condition that makes my heart too large. I was born with it. This condition has a bit of "medical fame." It has been associated with sudden death in young athletes. In my 30's, I had to have a defibrillator placed, and replaced approximately ten years later in my 40's. Even when medically necessary, we have pain after surgery. It's an assault on the body, albeit with a purpose. I am thankful for these scars. They play a part in hopefully giving me more decades on earth. The thing about these scars is they didn't just help me medically. I learned insight into what patients experienced. How IV contrast can make you feel like you just peed your pants, or how it can hurt even to turn to look at a friend after radiation to your neck due to the tightness from scar tissue.

I have greater empathy for my fellow patients. In this way, the concept of shared suffering can cause bonding and empathy for people who have also suffered, in the same way that you have suffered. There can sometimes be a danger in shared suffering where you lose empathy or make assumptions about people who have not suffered the same way you have—for example, in my situation. My cancer treatment involved an extensive process that was more than just the typical tonsillectomy. In addition to removing cancerous tonsils, I also had a lateral dissection into my neck with many lymph nodes removed, essentially two surgeries for one round of anesthesia. I had to follow it up with radiation to the neck and chemotherapy. Since my treatment and associated pain was more than a routine tonsillectomy, I could assume anyone with a "run-of-the-mill tonsillectomy" for non-cancerous reasons had it much easier. They "only" had their tonsils out without the additional surgery I endured. I could also minimize their pain and suffering since they only had one round of severe neck and throat pain instead of the multiple rounds I had. I had to not only heal from surgery and get over that pain but also go through the pain of chemo and radiation after each round of cancer. However, tonsillectomy is painful, and anyone who "only had a tonsillectomy" still experiences significant pain. This might seem silly, but there is a real-world analogy. My argument is even a person who's only experienced one of those things still deserves empathy. Suffering is not a competition. I hope we can learn to love each other enough to know that my suffering should not reduce my ability to empathize with someone who has suffered differently. I may not know your pain or have lived it. Sexual assault, domestic violence, racial injustice, losing a child, chronic pain, whatever your pain is, it matters. Is being a physician stressful? Yes, but so is working in child protection, flying airplanes, working on roofs, or being a business owner. Instead of competing with each other and maybe inadvertently sinking someone else's boat, let's love, heal, listen, and help everyone's hurt by creating a more loving world. After all, John F Kennedy said, "A rising tide lift's all boats." As Abraham Lincoln said, the alternative is that "A house divided against itself cannot stand." Well, it's often attributed to Lincoln, but like I said about perspective for all sides to understand truth, someone else said it first.

Maybe this white guy aches over Asian hate. Maybe this straight Christian guy aches for the hurt he has seen gay people face. Maybe one of my favorite Americans inspires me to listen more than I used to, to look for the light in others. Martin Luther King Jr. said, "Returning hate for hate multiplies hate, adding deeper darkness to a night already devoid of stars. Darkness cannot drive out darkness, only light can do that. Hate can not drive out hate, only love can do that."

Maybe I have friends who are cops and friends who spoke poorly about cops. Maybe I never was raped, but I spent years in college advocating for prevention and awareness about domestic violence and sexual assault. Maybe my hurt isn't yours, but we can heal each other. Maybe I wrote this book because my best friend died to save me from something I shouldn't have done. Maybe his hurting can heal us all.

I wish you the best in your healing journey. My friends, if there is anything I can pray about for you, let me know, after all, I am alive to write this book because of a prayer.

Endnotes

(1) Needtobreathe, Forever On Your Side, EP track #4 on *Forever on your side*, written by Bear Rinehart & Bo Rinehart, Atlantic Records, 2018, compact disc & vinyl.

(2) Hope Darst, Peace Be Still, track #5 on *Peace Be Still*, written by Hope Darst, Andrew Holt & Mia Fieldes, Fair Trade Services & Columbia, 2020, compact disc.

(3) King & Country, Cheering You On, track #12 on *What Are We Waiting For?* written by Josh Kerr, Jordan Reynolds, Luke Smallbone & Joel Smallbone, Word Entertainment & Curb Records, 2022, compact disc & vinyl.

(4) Martin Luther King Jr., *Strength to Love*, New York: Harper & Row, 1963.

(5) Jackie Robinson, Baseball America website -
https://www.baseballamerica.com/players/4888-jackie-robinson/

(6) 42, directed by Brian Helgeland (Warner Bros. Pictures, 2013), 2 hr., 8 min.

(7) Josh Hamilton, Baseball America website -
https://www.baseballamerica.com/players/5582-josh-hamilton/

(8) Needtobreathe, Hard Love, track #2 on *Hard Love*, written by Bear Rinehart & Bo Rinehart, Atlantic Records, 2016, compact disc & vinyl.

(9) Matthew West, Before You Ask Her, track #8 on *My Story Your Glory*, written by Matthew West, Reunion Records, 2023, compact disc.

(10) Miller Park is a retractable roof baseball park located in Milwaukee, Wisconsin. It is home to the Milwaukee Brewers and was completed in 2001 as a replacement for Milwaukee County Stadium.

(11) Cheesehead is a nickname in the United States for a person from Wisconsin or for a fan of the Green Bay Packers NFL football franchise.

(12) Garth Brooks, The Change, track #6 on *Fresh Horses*, written by Tony Arata & Wayne Tester, Capitol Nashville, 1995, compact disc.

(13) Corrie Ten Boom, *The Hiding Place*, Lincoln VA: Chosen Books, 1971.

(14) Alpha Course is an evangelistic course that seeks to introduce the basics of the Christian faith through a series of talks and discussions.

(15) Anne Wilson, Sunday Sermons, track #5 on *My Jesus*, written by Anne Wilson, Jeff Sojka & Ben Glover, Sparrow, 2022, compact disc.

(16) Minutemen were a small hand picked elite American fighting force, which were required to be highly mobile and able to assemble quickly.

(17) Randy Travis, Three Wooden Crosses, track #5 on *Rise and Shine*, written by Kim Williams & Doug Johnson, Word Records, 2002, compact disc.

(18) PRN (Latin phrase for 'pro re nata') meaning 'when required'

(19) Casting Crowns, Desert Road, track #1 on *Healer*, written by Mark Hall, Matthew West & Seth Mosley, Beach Street Records, 2022, compact disc.

(20) Top Gun, directed by Joseph Kosinski (Paramount Pictures, 2010), 2 hr., 10 min.

(21) Eric Clapton, My Father's Eyes, single and track #1 on *Pilgrim*, written by Eric Clapton, Reprise, Duck, 1998, compact disc.

(22) I Am They, Scars, track #4 on *Trial & Triumph*, written by Ethan Hulse, Jon McConnell, Matthew Armstrong & Matthew Hein, Essential, 2018, compact disc

Acknowledgments

Nobody hurts alone; nobody heals alone.

To the countless individuals who personally and professionally taught me healing scientifically, spiritually, socially, and individually, I am forever grateful. Some of you were formal mentors with official titles; many of you though were friends, family, patients, acquaintances, colleagues, even strangers. Some of you saw me on my best days; some of you on my worst days, but each of you matter. I saw you at work, at church, on the street, in my home, but most of all I feel you in my heart.

About the Author

Neal Boeder

Neal Boeder is an internal medicine physician, a two-time cancer survivor, and a dedicated father living in Minnesota. Born with a genetic heart condition, growing up on a farm and then living most of the past 20 years in the Twin Cities metro area has shaped his worldview. It allows him to relate to both "blue collar "and "white collar" worlds with humor and empathy. He values remaining humble, humorous, helping others, and the importance of hard work which his parents taught him.

After experiencing a miracle during his second cancer journey, Neal felt compelled to share his insights on healing. His debut book David Walking With Grace is a candid and refreshingly humorous account of his journey of recovery, science, and faith. He gives readers insight into all dimensions of "healing," including the physical, spiritual, emotional, and social aspects. He writes through the lens of physician, patient, and parent. He explores a wide range of conditions and experiences, from medical aspects such as cancer, pain, depression, and addiction, to life challenges such as divorce, societal divides, and abuse.

Neal hopes to help individuals, families, and society find ways to heal—to create a better world for future generations. Beyond his professional work, Neal volunteers his time, talents, and treasure into efforts and causes supporting children in third-world countries, as well as a diverse group of people in difficult circumstances in the U.S.

He prioritizes raising his daughter. She is a major inspiration for his writing. Neal hopes she leaves the world a little better than she found it. Being born during a total eclipse of the sun added a touch of cosmic wonder to his life. His genetic heart condition adds a reminder of our mortality. Neal has worked at multiple top hospitals and renowned healthcare systems.   Neal enjoys spending time with his family and friends. With a wide range of interests, his favorite aspect of his hobbies is getting to know people and their personal stories. During rare downtime alone he works on self-growth, enjoys comedy, and is mostly disappointed by his Minnesota sports teams.

www.ingramcontent.com/pod-product-compliance
Lightning Source LLC
La Vergne TN
LVHW051809080426
835513LV00017B/1874